CRAZYBALL

CRAZYBALL

Sports Scandals, Superstitions, and Sick Plays

Barry Wilner and Ken Rappoport

TAYLOR TRADE PUBLISHING
Lanham • Boulder • New York • Toronto • Plymouth, UK

Published by Taylor Trade Publishing
An imprint of Rowman & Littlefield
4501 Forbes Boulevard, Suite 200, Lanham, Maryland 20706
www.rowman.com

10 Thornbury Road, Plymouth PL6 7PP, United Kingdom

Distributed by National Book Network

British Library Cataloguing in Publication Information Available

Library of Congress Cataloging-in-Publication Data
Wilner, Barry.
Crazyball : sports scandals, superstitions, and sick plays / Barry Wilner and Ken Rappoport.
pages cm.
ISBN 978-1-58979-912-7 (pbk. : alk. paper) — ISBN 978-1-58979-913-4 (electronic)
1. Sports—Miscellanea. 2. Sports—History. I. Rappoport, Ken. II. Title.
GV707.W53 2014
796—dc23
2014001558

∞™ The paper used in this publication meets the minimum requirements of American National Standard for Information Sciences Permanence of Paper for Printed Library Materials, ANSI/NISO Z39.48-1992.

Printed in the United States of America

CONTENTS

PROLOGUE

In a sometimes crazy world, sports contribute more than their share of craziness.

Welcome to *Crazyball*, a collection of the greatest and most unusual sports stories ever told.

From the Black Sox to bounty hunters, the Marx Brothers to Wrong Way Riegels, *Crazyball* is all over the place, featuring an endless supply of off-the-wall moments in sports.

Try Evel Knievel's aborted leap across Snake Canyon. The wild and crazy antics of mascots from the San Diego Chicken to the Phillie Phanatic. How about the great double-talkers, from Casey Stengel to Yogi Berra?

You want more crazy?

Remember the All-American Red Heads, the female version of the Harlem Globetrotters?

The authors, longtime sports writers with The Associated Press, also focus on other crazy moments in sports history: the worst scandals and the most numerous pranks, famous botched plays, and laughable losers of all time.

Oh, yes, the authors have also included the most outrageously funny sports movies of all time. See if you don't agree.

1

SPORTS' WORST TEAMS

OR ON A CLEAR DAY, YOU CAN SEE 11TH PLACE

OK, so most everyone agrees the expansion New York Mets of 1962 is the worst team in Major League Baseball history. Well, not exactly.

Sure, the "Amazin' Mets" went 40-120 to set a modern record for futility in the 20th century.

But compared to the Cleveland Spiders of 1899, the Mets were the '98 Yankees.

How bad were the Spiders that year?

So bad they needed psychiatric counseling.

So bad they weren't able to finish out the season.

So bad they played most games on the road because fans weren't coming to home games.

Could you blame the fans? Their indifference was fueled by a pitiful 20-134 record.

Seriously: 20-134.

The Spiders' story began in a different era when baseball owners could own more than one team. That's where the trouble started for Spiders owner Frank Robison. He had made his fortune in trolley cars, but clearly was on the wrong track with this Spiders team.

Robison was unhappy with fan support in Cleveland during the 1898 season. Despite an 81-68 record, the Spiders only drew 70,496. After the season, Robison bought the bankrupt St. Louis Browns and shipped his best players to the Browns, now renamed the Perfectos. Robison figured his new team would get better fan support in St. Louis.

One of the players who remained in Cleveland was second baseman Joe Quinn, who doubled as manager. Quinn was an undertaker by trade. When the Spiders got off to an 8-30 start, sports writers cracked that Quinn was now in charge of 20 stiffs.

The Spiders naturally finished 12th in the 12-team National League. They hit rock bottom in one game when only 95 patrons showed up. During the season, the Spiders were known by various nicknames: The Leftovers, Wanderers, Misfits, Forlorns, Forsakers, Outcasts, Tramps, Exiles, Cast-offs, Excursionists, Orphans, and, whew, Tailenders.

As you can imagine, the '89 Spiders posted some amazing negative streaks, including 24 losses in a row at one point, still a big-league record. Winning streaks? They only had one, for two games.

In St. Louis, despite fielding some of the most talented players in the big leagues, including Hall of Famers Cy Young and Jesse Burkett, the Browns/Perfectos managed just a fifth-place finish.

They did fill the seats, though, drawing 373,909. That was good for second in the league.

THE BAKER BOYS

By some estimates, the Philadelphia Phillies were the first professional sports franchise to reach the 10,000-loss mark. It took them more than 125 years of mostly incredibly terrible baseball to, uh, *earn* that dubious distinction.

During the 1920s and 1930s, the luckless Phillies played in Baker Bowl. One of the ballpark's most distinctive traits was a giant soap advertisement in right field:

"The Phillies Use Lifebuoy."

You wouldn't have blamed fans if they had added the postscript:

"And they still stink."

WAKE-UP CALL

Baker Bowl was quirky. In right field a lining of tin covered a 40-foot brick wall. When balls hit the wall, a loud clanking sound echoed throughout the ballpark.

One July afternoon in 1934, the Brooklyn club was in town to play the Phillies. Walter Beck, a mediocre pitcher at best, was on the mound for the Dodgers. Although Beck held the lead, Brooklyn manager Casey Stengel decided to lift the pitcher.

Beck was not happy. He wound up and fired the ball at the tin-lined fence in right field, some 280 feet away.

Brooklyn right fielder Hack Wilson, recovering from a long night of carousing, had closed his eyes at precisely that moment.

When the ball slammed against the wall, Wilson woke up in a hurry.

Wilson sprung into action. He fielded the ball cleanly, turned and fired to second base. Only then did the Hall of Fame outfielder realize what had happened. Chagrined, he went back to his position.

"There is no record of whether the phantom runner was called safe or out," reported one sports writer.

RED-FACED

It was during a game in Cincinnati when the New York Mets' 1962 season was defined by one play.

Mets centerfielder Richie Ashburn wanted to make sure he and Venezuelan shortstop Elio Chacon had their signals straight on coverage of fly balls in shallow left-center field. Chacon was the kind of shortstop who claimed most anything in the air, no matter where the ball was hit.

So before the game, Ashburn asked a bilingual teammate how to say "I got it" in Spanish. "*Yo la tengo*," he was told.

So here comes a pop fly, and there goes Chacon after the ball.

"I see him whipping out from shortstop like a little kid on a scooter," Ashburn once recalled. "So I yell, '*Yo la tengo*! *Yo la tengo*!'"

So Chacon pulled up.

Frank Thomas didn't. Clearly Thomas didn't speak Spanish. He steamrolled into Ashburn, knocking the ball loose.

Just another mistake in a season of miscues for one of baseball's all-time worst teams—210 errors, to be exact.

ALL BAD THINGS COME TO AN END

The 1962 season couldn't end quickly enough for the Mets. Appropriately, they helped things along by hitting into a triple play in the final game of the season in Chicago.

Afterward, manager Casey Stengel surveyed the damage.

"This was a group effort," Stengel told his assembled players in a somber locker room. "No one player could have done all this."

Stengel was asked by a newspaperman if the season had been any fun.

"I would have to say no to that one," the manager said.

DOUBLE TALK

Casey Stengel was totally aware of the lack of talent when he took over as manager of the New York Mets in 1962. This is what he advised his outfielders:

"When one of them hits a single to you, throw the ball to third. That way we can hold them to a double."

BIG MISTAKE

Following the New York Yankees' loss to Pittsburgh in the 1960 World Series, the team fired the 70-year-old Stengel.

Too old, the Yankees said.

Stengel had an answer for that.

"I'll never make the mistake of being 70 again."

UNKIND TO KINER

With a 42-112 record, the 1952 Pittsburgh Pirates represented the worst baseball team in the city's history. One of the few bright lights: slugger Ralph Kiner, who led the National League in home runs for the seventh straight year.

Although Kiner was the most popular player in town, it did not earn him a pay raise from general manager Branch Rickey, called "El Cheapo" for his tightfisted money habits. Following the '52 season, Rickey sent Kiner a contract with a 25 percent pay cut.

Kiner, who was making $90,000, expected a raise, not a cut.

A contract battle continued for several months. Finally, Rickey flew to Los Angeles to talk contract with his unhappy star.

"Where did we finish last year?" Rickey asked Kiner.

"Last."

"Well, we can finish last without you."

Kiner took the cut.

NO PAT ON THE BACK

With its schedule of 162 games, baseball has had more of an opportunity than most sports to produce some stinkers. That hasn't stopped the 1976 Tampa Bay Buccaneers from looking ridiculously inept in their first three years in the National Football League.

For all the success that John McKay had coaching Southern Cal football, his pro career was a flop by comparison. In his first season at Tampa Bay, McKay's team went 0-14. The

Bucs extended the losing streak to 26 in the second year before they finally won a game.

Depression set in early for McKay after a number of injuries had prevented the Bucs from being competitive.

What did the coach do?

"The coach stopped talking to us," defensive lineman Pat Toomey told the *Columbus Dispatch* in 2001.

McKay continued to drop one-liners, though. Asked by a newspaperman what he thought of his team's execution, McKay replied:

"I think it's a good idea."

AT A LOSS FOR WORDS

Then there's the NBA's embarrassment, the 1972–73 Philadelphia 76ers. Fred Carter was chosen the 76ers' most valuable player, although valuable was a relative term after a horrendous 9-73 year.

"I don't know if it was for leading the team to nine wins or for leading the team to 73 losses," Carter said. "How could we have an MVP? I didn't lead us anywhere. I was embarrassed to be the MVP."

The longest-suffering team in NBA history was filled with memorable stories and quirky characters, one of them the colorful John Q. Trapp.

During one game, 76ers coach Roy Rubin wanted to substitute for Trapp. The player shook his head "no" and looked into the stands. A friend of Trapp opened his jacket to reveal a revolver.

Needless to say, Trapp stayed in the game.

A LOSING EFFORT

Let's not leave hockey out of the discussion. Take the 1974–75 Washington Capitals—something just about everyone managed to do on the scoreboard.

After they won their first road game of the season, Garnett (Ace) Bailey grabbed a garbage can in the locker room. He scribbled his name on it and pranced around the dressing room, holding it overhead like a Stanley Cup.

Small wonder. The worst NHL team in history (8-67-5) had suffered 37 straight road defeats before finally winning one, 5-3 over Oakland on March 28.

"That was a scary team, real scary," said Ron Low, the Capitals' first goaltender, who spent many a night in tears. "We were a small team and got pushed around by just about everybody."

Bailey had been a Stanley Cup winner in Boston. So he was given the privilege to carry the "Cup" around the dressing room that day.

The fun didn't last long. The Caps reverted to form in the final games of their expansion season to finish with a horrible 1-39 road mark.

AIR BALL

Not even the Washington Generals were this bad. The well-known whipping boys of the Harlem Globetrotters have been used to losing on a regular basis, but Cal Tech outdid even them.

From 1996 to 2007, Cal Tech's basketball team lost 207 games in a row.

Repeat: *207 in a row.*

And when they won?

"They were euphoric," said coach Roy Dow of Cal Tech after the Beavers won their first NCAA game in 11 years by defeating Bard College of New York 81-52 in January 2007.

Although the school has a number of athletic programs, you might have guessed that Cal Tech is more concerned with turning out Nobel Prize winners than NBA players. This the school has done more than 30 times.

"You wonder about the wisdom of passing out swords to the Cal Tech fencing squad," observed one sports writer. "You have to hope the kids at Cal Tech sword-fight better than they play basketball. Otherwise, it could be dangerous."

Among other colleges, Northwestern was also known for monster losing streaks. From 1979–1982, the Wildcats lost 34 straight football games, including a 61-14 home loss to Michigan State. Northwestern students went wild after another thumping. They tore down the goalposts and marched through town shouting, "We're the worst!"

FABULOUS FANS

Philadelphia is known for sports fans who love to boo. It's something that's usually foreign to fans in Cleveland, despite a history of mostly bad sports moments.

The latest: 26 straight losses by the Cavaliers in the 2011 season that tied the NFL's Tampa Bay Buccaneers for the longest losing streak in North American major pro team sports.

The streak didn't bother fans at the Quicken Loans Arena in downtown Cleveland. They continued to maintain their undying loyalty despite the season-long lack of success.

While the Cavs were on their way to their latest defeat, a woman in the second deck wiggled and bounced around, screaming again and again, "Don't give up, Cleveland." She flashed a cardboard sign that read, DON'T GIVE UP, CLEVELAND!

She continued her tirade even after the game was over and another loss was planted in the books.

"Don't give up, Cleveland, we all love you!" she shrieked, adding the postscript, according to one newspaper, "even though you stink."

THE CURSE OF CLEVELAND

The Catch. The Shot. The Drive. The Decision.

Then there was The Move.

Cleveland's sports fans have suffered through a never-ending number of heartbreaking moments, on and off the field. Before Art Modell moved the Browns out of Cleveland in 1995 and LeBron James left for Miami in 2010, there was plenty for Cleveland sports fans to be miserable about.

Try these three, just a small sampling of historic frustrations dating from the 1950s:

First, The Catch.

The Indians were tied with the New York Giants in the eighth inning of Game 1 of the 1954 World Series. There were two men on base when Vic Wertz stepped to the plate.

Wertz smashed a towering drive to center field. Two runs, easy. Center field at the Polo Grounds was some 500 feet away, the longest from home plate in baseball. The ball could roll forever.

That is, unless the outfielder playing center field for the Giants was Willie Mays.

Back, back, back went Mays.

The runners were on their way home. Suddenly, they were on their way back. With Mays's back to the plate, he had somehow caught up with the ball with an over-the-shoulder basket catch. After the ball settled into Mays's glove, he quickly turned and fired toward the plate, preventing any runs from scoring. It was the defining play of Mays's Hall of Fame career.

The Giants went on to win the game in extra innings and completed a four-game sweep of the Indians, who had incidentally won an American League–record 111 games.

The Shot: Another defining moment for an athletic great at the expense of a Cleveland team.

This time it was the first round of the 1989 NBA playoffs, Michael Jordan's Chicago Bulls against the Cavaliers. The teams had split the first four games, the fifth and deciding game due up at Cleveland's Richfield Coliseum.

The Bulls trailed the Cavs for the entire game, until Jordan hit a shot to put Chicago ahead, 99-98, with six seconds left.

Back came the Cavs on a driving shot by Craig Ehlo to go ahead once more, 100-99.

Three seconds left.

With Ehlo racing after Jordan, the Bulls' star double-pumped a 15-footer to give the Bulls a 101-100 victory that knocked the Cavaliers out of the playoffs. The Shot killed any chances that year for the Cavs, who had one of their best basketball teams in the city's history.

The Bulls would soon be on their way to a dynasty.

Typical Cleveland.

The Drive: Mention John Elway in Denver and fans still remember the late drive that helped pull out the AFC championship game in January 1987, ending in another frustrating defeat for the Browns.

With 5:32 left, the Browns were up 20-13 and nearing a shot at their first Super Bowl. The Cleveland crowd was smelling blood.

The Browns kicked off and the Broncos botched the return, leaving the ball on Denver's 2-yard line.

First down, 98 yards to go.

A tough situation for Elway? No problem. Time to do it his way. And for Clevelanders to be disappointed again.

In what has become an iconic moment in NFL history, Elway put together an almost-perfect touchdown drive that tied the game, 20-20, with 39 seconds left in regulation. Along the way, the Denver quarterback completed a clutch, 20-yard pass on third-and-18.

In overtime, it was Elway again to the rescue as he led a 60-yard drive that finished with a winning field goal by the Broncos' Rich Karlis.

That was bad enough. The worst was yet to come for the Browns, only this time it happened off the field, when owner Art Modell moved the team to Baltimore in 1995.

A new Browns team was eventually formed in Cleveland and began play in 1999. Things hadn't changed. The remodeled Browns were still looking for the city's first league championship in any sport since the 1960s. Cleveland came close when James led the Cavs to the NBA Finals before "taking his talents" to South Beach.

Old habits never die. Especially losing habits.

2

BOTCHBALL

Screwups happen, even to Hall of Fame players.

The passage of time hasn't helped many great athletes whose boneheaded plays lasted long after their careers were over.

As a member of the notorious Purple People Eaters, Jim Marshall set National Football League records of 302 consecutive games played and 30 fumbles recovered. Ironically, it was one particular fumble recovery he made in 1964 for which he's most remembered, and not in a positive way.

Welcome "Wrong Way" Marshall.

Marshall's goof was hardly unique in the world of sports.

Consider Roy Riegels, another football star from a different era who also screwed up big-time. And he's not alone.

Fred Merkle, Mickey Owen, Bill Buckner, Chris Webber, Fred Brown, Joe Pisarcik, Jack Dempsey, even the great Babe Ruth, are remembered in ways they'd prefer not to be memorialized.

Marshall starred at Columbus East High School in Ohio and ran with a dangerous crowd. "Half the guys I grew up with are in the Ohio Penitentiary," he said in a *New York Times* interview.

He was an All-American at Ohio State, skipping out a year early to play for Saskatchewan in the Canadian Football League "because someone offered me $10,000."

Two years later, he was playing—and starring—for the Minnesota Vikings.

Off the field, life was often unsettling.

In the winter of 1971 Marshall was lost in a blizzard with friends on a snowmobile expedition. He managed to survive by burning money and credit cards to keep warm. They were found by rescuers, but one in the party died of exposure.

Certainly Marshall had to be one of the most interesting and colorful football players in NFL history, ready to accept any kind of challenge on or off the field. You name it, Marshall tried it: skydiving, scuba diving, studying Zen Buddhism, archery. To Vikings coach Bud Grant, Marshall was the Vikings' most consistent, hard-working player.

"We take Jim for granted," Grant once said of Marshall, "and that's been our luxury."

Grant's favorite Marshall play occurred in the snow during a game against Detroit. Marshall had recovered a fumble and was tackled from behind. As he was going down, he flipped the ball backward into the hands of teammate Alan Page. Page scored a touchdown.

"There was no way he could have seen Page," Grant said in amazement. "He told me that he just knew Page would be there."

In 1964, Marshall was having a pretty good game against San Francisco until his goof in the fourth quarter in Kezar Stadium. The Vikings led the 49ers 27-17 when San Francisco's George Mira passed to Billy Kilmer over the middle with 8:12 left.

Kilmer fumbled and Marshall picked up the loose ball, "and took off running."

The crowd went wild.

Marshall was running in the wrong direction.

"Everyone was waving and shouting, but I thought they were cheering me on," Marshall said.

Vikings quarterback Fran Tarkenton was running on the sideline shouting at his teammate. Marshall thought Tarkenton was encouraging him to run even faster.

When he reached the Vikings' own end zone and heaved the ball into the stands, he realized something was wrong, *very* wrong.

"I had never heard a crowd react that way," he said. "Then I turned and saw some of my teammates pointing back the other way. My spirits just sank."

The San Francisco players were loving it. After Marshall tossed the ball away for a 2-point safety, 49ers center Bruce Bosley ran up to Marshall, grabbed his hands, hugged him, and said thanks.

Despite the screwup, the Vikings held on for a 27-22 victory.

"Little kids who weren't even born back then will come and say, 'You're the guy that ran the wrong way,'" Marshall said. "It's a hell of a thing to be known for, isn't it?"

WRONG WAY RIEGELS

Roy Riegels was about to become a part of football lore.

The date: January 1, 1929.

The place: Pasadena, California.

The event: The Rose Bowl

A capacity crowd of some 70,000 crowded into the massive Rose Bowl stadium in 80-degree weather to watch a post-season clash between two of the nation's football titans. It was California's Golden Bears against the Georgia Tech Yellow Jackets in a matchup of teams from the West and East. At the time the Rose Bowl was the only major bowl game in the country in an era when college football was king.

It also was an era when football meant playing both ways. For many, that meant staying on the field for the full 60 minutes, no matter the players' state of exhaustion.

Riegels, an All-American, was a featured player at center and linebacker. He had led the Bears in minutes played during a 6-1-2 season. He figured to see plenty of action against a fine Georgia Tech team that had gone 9-0 during the regular season and was gunning for the national championship.

One sports writer said the game "may be decided on breaks." It was, but no one expected the kind of break that Georgia Tech got in the closing minutes of the first half.

The teams went scoreless in the first quarter before Riegels's misstep in the second.

Georgia Tech had the ball in the vicinity of its 30-yard line when John Thomason, nicknamed "Stumpy," was hammered by California's Benny Lom and fumbled. Riegels scooped up the ball and took off for the Georgia Tech end zone. Suddenly, he spun around to avoid tacklers and headed in the other direction—toward his own goal line.

"I was running toward the sidelines when I picked up the ball," Riegels later told The Associated Press. "I started to turn to my left toward Tech's goal. Somebody shoved me and I bounded right off into a tackler. In pivoting to get away from him, I completely lost my bearings."

And broadcaster Graham McNamee thought he had completely lost his mind.

"What am I seeing?" McNamee said while calling the game on radio. "Am I crazy? Am I crazy? Am I crazy?"

Say the same for the stunned crowd and players. For a while, the players didn't know what to do. Everyone, that is, but Lom. California's star halfback took off after the misguided Riegels.

"Stop! Stop! You're going the wrong way!" Lom shouted at his teammate as he streaked downfield.

Riegels shrugged off his teammate, according to one account.

"As we neared the [California] goal line," Riegels said, "I thought I heard Benny shouting for me to throw him the ball. I wasn't going to throw it to him after that run."

Finally, he realized something was wrong when Lom tackled him on the 1-yard line. The terrible truth dawned on Riegels as teammates gathered around to console him. Riegels, his head buried in his hands, just wanted to dig a hole on the Rose Bowl turf and crawl in.

The Bears soon went into punt formation. Riegels snapped the ball to Lom, but his punt was blocked. Cal's Stan Barr was the last player to touch the ball before it rolled out of the end zone for a safety. Georgia Tech went into the locker room holding a 2-0 lead.

"The same team will start the second half," California coach Clarence "Nibs" Price told his players. Everyone responded—with the exception of Riegels. Price wanted to know what was wrong.

"Coach, I can't do it," said Riegels, tears streaming down his face. "I've ruined you, I've ruined myself, I've ruined the University of California. I couldn't face that crowd to save my life."

Price put his hand on Riegels's shoulder.

"Get up and go back out there," the coach said. "The game is only half over."

Riegels responded with a ferocious second half that impressed Georgia Tech, blocking a punt at one point. One Yellow Jackets player said Riegels was the best lineman he had faced all year.

It wasn't enough for California. The Bears gave up a touchdown that dropped them eight points behind Georgia Tech. The Golden Bears came up with a TD in the final two minutes, cutting the Yellow Jackets' lead to 8-7.

That's how it ended, with Riegels's gaffe the deciding margin in the game.

It didn't affect the way his teammates felt about him. The following season, Riegels was chosen team captain and also was selected to All-America teams while leading the Golden Bears to a 7-1-1 record.

Following graduation, Riegels coached football, served as an officer in the Army Air Corps during World War II, and owned a fertilizer business in California. In 1991, two years before his death, Riegels was inducted into the Rose Bowl Hall of Fame.

Through the years Riegels accepted his infamous role in football mythology with dignity and grace. At a Georgia Tech Letterman's Club meeting in 1971 honoring the 1928 team, Riegels was presented with an honorary membership card.

"Believe me, I feel I've earned this," joked the man, fairly or unfairly, who would forever be known as Wrong Way Riegels.

MERKLE'S BONER

Definition of a bonehead:

Someone who pulls a boner, makes a foolish mistake; i.e., "The manager pulled a boner and lost the game."

In this case, it was a player, not the manager, responsible for the boner. His name, Fred Merkle.

"I wish folks would forget, but they never will," said the former New York baseball player who was accused by some of costing the Giants the pennant in 1908.

Before his death in 1956, Merkle was still lamenting his frivolous fate. "I suppose the epitaph on my tombstone will read, 'Here lies Bonehead Merkle.'"

Merkle was tormented by his mistake for nearly 50 years, constantly reminded of it. No place was safe. Once attending church services in Florida with his family in the 1930s, Merkle was talking to a visiting minister.

"You don't know me," the minister said, "but you know where I'm from! Toledo, Ohio! The hometown of Bonehead Fred Merkle."

Born December 20, 1888, in Watertown, Wisconsin, the son of German immigrants, Merkle grew up in Toledo, where he starred regionally in baseball and football. Merkle's standout play in various semi-pro and minor leagues alerted the Giants, who bought his contract for $2,500.

In a major league baseball career that extended from 1907 to 1926, most of it with the Giants, the slick-fielding first baseman was anything but a bonehead. He sported a solid .273 career batting average with 82 home runs, most of them in the Dead Ball Era. He also drove in 733 runs and stole 272 bases.

It was September 23, 1908, when Merkle became a part of baseball mythology.

Baseball is a sport defined in many ways by controversies. This was one for the ages. It came smack in the middle of a torrid pennant race between the Giants, the Chicago Cubs, and the Pittsburgh Pirates.

The Giants and the Cubs in particular were considered baseball's finest in that era. Their battles for the pennant were compelling, the Giants winning the pennant in 1904 and 1905, the Cubs in 1906 and 1907.

Now the teams were meeting in another typical late-season battle, this one in the Polo Grounds in Upper Manhattan. Giants manager John McGraw made one important change in his lineup, inserting the 19-year-old rookie Merkle at first base to replace the injured Fred Tenney.

Merkle, starting his first game of the season, had signed with the Giants the year before and had been used sparingly by McGraw.

The Giants-Cubs contest late in the '08 season was a classic low-scoring, high-tension game. The teams were tied 1-1 with two outs in the bottom of the ninth. New York had runners at the corners, Harry McCormick at third base, and Merkle at first.

Al Bridewell drove a pitch from Jack Pfiester into right-center field for a single. McCormick raced home with the winning run for the Giants.

Or did he?

While bedlam erupted at the Polo Grounds with an apparent Giants victory, Merkle took off for the clubhouse in center field. It was common practice at the conclusion of games at the Polo Grounds for players to run straight for the clubhouse to escape the boisterous crowds.

In so doing, Merkle had forgotten one simple act that would have clinched the victory for the Giants: He never touched second base. So technically the force was still on.

As the *New York Times* reported:

> McCormick trots home, the merry villagers flock on the field to worship the hollow where the great [Christy] Mathewson's feet have pressed, and all of a sudden there is doings at second base.

Mathewson, the Giants' star pitcher, was in fact trying to maneuver Merkle back on the field so he could touch second.

Meanwhile, Cubs second baseman Johnny Evers was involved in a drama of his own on the infield dirt. Evers was calling for center fielder "Circus Solly" Hoffman to throw him the ball so he could step on the bag for the forceout, thus eliminating the Giants' run.

There is some suspicion that, in the melee that ensued, it may not have been the actual ball that was originally in play.

But Evers nevertheless stepped on second for the force. Then he started arguing vehemently with the umpires that Merkle should have been called out and the Giants' run nullified.

Despite the confused circumstances, most of the fans went home that day believing the Giants had won and stretched their lead over the Cubs to two games. It was only after newspapers came out the following day that all of New York's sports fans went into mourning: The umpires and National League president Harry Pulliam supported Evers's claim.

The game was officially recorded as a 1-1 tie and would only be replayed if the Cubs and Giants were tied at the end of the season.

Which is exactly what happened.

This time, the Cubs took down the great Mathewson to finish with their third straight pennant. Then they beat the Detroit Tigers for their last world championship.

Merkle went on to play on three straight pennant winners and in five World Series, but never lived down his infamous boner. Bridewell felt for his teammate, as did others.

"I wish I had never gotten that hit," Bridewell said years later. "It would have saved Fred from a lot of unfair humiliation."

TWO FOR THE SHOW

Talk about dropping the ball.

Talking about it for years. In fact, still talking about it.

Mickey Owen wished it would go away.

So does Bill Buckner.

For Owen, it happened in the 1941 World Series. For Buckner, the 1986 World Series.

In both cases, blunders led to their teams losing the championship.

Owen's Brooklyn Dodgers were still looking for their first World Series championship, while Buckner's Boston Red Sox hadn't won the title since 1918.

For Owen and Buckner, their fatal mistakes overshadowed notable careers.

Everyone remembers Owen's infamous blunder. Few recall he was a four-time all-star, perhaps the best defensive catcher in the game in his time. The sturdy Brooklyn backstop set a National League single-season record in 1941 by handling 476 consecutive chances *without an error*. Remarkably, Owen only made three errors in 597 chances over the entire season.

Owen, who broke into the major leagues with the St. Louis Cardinals, was no stranger to records. In 1942, he became the first player to pinch-hit a homer in the All-Star Game.

Owen was part of a strong Dodgers team that featured National League batting leader Pete Reiser and home run and RBI leader Dolph Camilli. They were only a small part of the best Brooklyn team in twenty years.

"No one man carried our club," Camilli said. "We all had great years."

Until the 1941 season, the Dodgers had gone through two decades of mediocrity following a pennant winner in 1920. Their World Series opponents, the New York Yankees, had won four straight championships before a momentary setback in 1940. In 1941 they stormed back to snatch the American League pennant behind the slugging of Joe DiMaggio, Tommy Heinrich, and Charlie Keller.

With the Dodgers edging the St. Louis Cardinals in a down-to-the-wire race for the National League pennant, the 1941 season did not lack for melodrama. The Yankees won the American League pennant going away and also produced the league MVP in DiMaggio, who set a record by hitting in 56 straight games. Boston's Ted Williams finished the year at .406, setting a standard for years to come.

A fascinating season, to be sure. Ah, but there were other noteworthy events to follow in the World Series.

The Yankees had won two of the first three games, but the Dodgers were about to square it in Game 4 at Ebbets Field in Brooklyn. They led 4-3 in the ninth and only needed one out to make it 2-2.

On the mound for the Dodgers: Hugh Casey, who had won 14 games and saved seven others during the season with one of the best curveballs in baseball.

At bat for the Yankees: Tommy Heinrich, the outfielder otherwise known as "Old Reliable."

With nobody on base and two outs, Casey went to a 3-2 count.

As Owen once recalled that fateful day:

"Casey had two curves. He had the big sweeping curve he'd tried a couple of times earlier in the game, but it had hung. Then he had the quick curve which was working real good. When I called for the curve, I was looking for the quick one, but Casey rolled off that big one, and it really broke."

Heinrich swung and missed.

Third out, game over.

Well, not quite.

A surprised Owen wasn't able to get his glove down in time. The ball bounced off the heel and rolled over to the Brooklyn dugout. By the time Owen retrieved the ball, there was no play on Heinrich at first.

"That ball broke like nothing I had ever seen Casey throw," Heinrich said. "That thing broke so sharp that as I tried to hold up, my mind said, 'He [Owen] might have trouble with it.'"

With Heinrich standing on first, the Yankees still had life.

They punched across four runs as DiMaggio singled, Keller doubled, Bill Dickey walked, and Joe Gordon doubled. The Yankees won 7-4 and wrapped up the series the next day with a 3-1 victory over the Dodgers.

Casey was furious following Owen's missed third strike. Strangely, no one went out to the mound to calm him after Heinrich reached first—not Dodgers manager Leo Durocher, and not Owen.

"I guess I should have [gone to the mound]," Owen said. "But I was a young catcher [25 at the time], and in a state of shock. I just went blank."

Following his Dodgers stint, Owen played four more seasons in the majors with the Chicago Cubs and Boston Red Sox, and three in the ill-fated Mexican League before retiring after the 1954 season.

Owen subsequently worked as a scout, then founded the Mickey Owen Baseball School in Miller, Missouri, to develop young players. Owen also served as the sheriff in his native southwest Missouri.

Whenever attention was drawn to his infamous flub, Owen responded good-naturedly.

"I don't mind being the goat," he said. "I'm just sorry for what I cost the other players."

The World Series share for the winning Yankees was $5,943; the losers share for the Dodgers, $4,829.

Around his home in Missouri, Owen was always a popular figure until his death at the age of 89. Everyone would gather around to hear his stories, and Owen had quite a story to tell them.

BILLY GOAT

"The one thing Buckner has is a soft pair of hands," Boston Red Sox manager John McNamara said of first baseman Bill Buckner. "He catches what he gets to."

Well, not always. And there was one blunder on baseball's biggest stage that would never be forgotten.

Buckner's egregious gaffe overshadowed a respectable 20-year career in the majors: 2,715 hits, including 174 home runs, for a lifetime batting average of .289. He also played in an All-Star Game and two World Series.

Before Buckner arrived in Boston in 1984, the California native had already established himself with the Los Angeles Dodgers and Chicago Cubs as a dependable hitter and fielder at three positions: left field, right field, and first base. With the Cubs in 1980, Buckner led the National League in batting with a .324 average.

"Too many good things happened to me," Buckner said, "a lot of good things."

Yes, but one bad mistake erased them all for Red Sox fans.

It was Game 6 of the 1986 World Series at Shea Stadium in New York. Buckner's Red Sox were one out away from winning their first World Series since 1918. They led the New York Mets 5-3 in the 10th, two outs and nobody on, reliever Calvin Schiraldi on the mound.

Suddenly things came unraveled for the Red Sox. Schiraldi gave up three straight singles to cut Boston's lead to 5-4 with runners at first and third.

In came Bob Stanley to face Mookie Wilson. The count went to 2-and-2. The Red Sox were now one strike away from winning the Series.

Not so fast. Stanley threw a wild pitch, allowing the Mets to tie the game, 5-5.

Then, on the 10th pitch thrown to him, Wilson slapped a grounder toward the first base bag. Buckner, playing deep, raced over to the line. Too late. The ball squirted between his legs, allowing Ray Knight to score the winning run and keep the Mets alive in the series.

For a while the shocking loss didn't seem to affect the Red Sox. They had a three-run lead in Game 7, but the Mets rallied to win the championship.

Unforgiving Red Sox fans, simmering with years of frustration, made Buckner the target of their wrath. Because of the ill will he generated, he eventually was forced to move his family out of town.

"At least once a week during the season, something is said. Why put up with it? I'm tired of it," Buckner said in explaining why he moved.

Buckner was soon gone from the Red Sox, as well, when they released him the following year. He signed as a free agent with the California Angels. Buckner finished out his career with a short stint in Kansas City, following a brief revisit with the Red Sox.

In his final short-lived appearance in Boston in 1990 he was given a standing ovation by the fans. It didn't do anything to assuage his bitter feelings about being singled out as the goat of the 1986 World Series.

Perhaps others might be just as deserving, especially Schiraldi and Stanley, who pitched ineffectively in late-inning relief roles. Remember, Red Sox pitchers failed to hold a three-run lead in Game 7.

But right or wrong, it was Buckner who would always wear the goat horns.

A GIANT MISTAKE

"Just fall on it."

The players in the New York Giants' huddle fully expected quarterback Joe Pisarcik to make the obvious call to take a knee in a 1978 game against the Philadelphia Eagles.

That's all that was needed for a routine 17-12 victory over the Eagles that would keep the Giants' playoff hopes alive. They had the ball on their 29 with only 31 seconds left. The Eagles were out of timeouts and the last play of the game was obvious.

Take a knee and let time run out, right?

Wrong.

Bob Gibson, the Giants' offensive coordinator, was thinking otherwise. He called for "Pro Up 65," a handoff to fullback Larry Csonka, even though Csonka had told Pisarcik, "Don't give me the football."

Noted Giants center Jim Clack:

"There was total chaos in the huddle. No one was sure what was going on."

There was more dysfunction at the line of scrimmage, as Pisarcik mishandled the football. It bounced off Csonka's hip and fell to the turf.

Philadelphia cornerback Herman Edwards picked up the fumble and raced into the end zone.

Shockingly, the Eagles had pulled out a miraculous 19-17 victory in a game they had all but lost. To Eagles fans, it would forever be known as "The Miracle at the Meadowlands." For Giants fans, "The Fumble."

The loss killed all playoff hopes for the Giants while the Eagles went on to the postseason.

It figured. If any team was going to lose a game like that it would be the luckless Giants, who were going through a streak of lousy football teams and terrible seasons.

Pisarcik got another chance when he joined the Eagles as a backup quarterback in 1980 and played there before he retired in 1984. Pisarcik, who became a financial adviser following his retirement from football, said he learned a lot about himself from the fumble.

"Something to be learned from this play is that what seems to be important in life is not what happened but how you react to what happened. Do you go home and forget about it? Does it make you stronger? It made me stronger."

SUPER DUPER MISTAKES

Mardi Gras in New Orleans, as wild as it comes.

But what could be more outrageous than what happened at the Superdome at the NCAA's Final Four in 1982 and 1993?

For both Chris Webber and Fred Brown, it was all too much crazyball.

They made mistakes—big ones. And the mistakes each time handed the national basketball championship to Dean Smith's North Carolina Tar Heels. In Brown's case, it was literal.

Smith had been to six previous Final Fours and come home without the championship trophy each time. And now it seemed he was destined for another failure when Eric "Sleepy" Floyd hit a jump shot to give Georgetown a 62-61 lead with 57 seconds left.

Smith called timeout and drew up the play: Kill the clock for one last shot. James Worthy was the logical choice to take it—he had already scored a career-high 28 points for the Tar Heels.

But instead Smith designed the play for freshman Michael Jordan. With 18 seconds remaining, Jordan hit a jumper from 16 feet to give the Tar Heels a 63-62 lead.

"I didn't see it go in," Jordan said. "I was just praying it would go. I never did look at the ball."

Now there were eight seconds left, the Hoyas controlling the ball. Brown, one of the country's top point guards, spotted an open teammate on the wing.

He passed to his right.

"I tried to pass to Eric Smith," Brown said. "It wasn't him."

Wrong man. It was Worthy, who gathered the ball to his chest. The Tar Heels star was fouled on the play and missed two shots, but it didn't matter. The Tar Heels had a one-point victory and Smith had his first national championship on his seventh try.

Brown would contribute to Georgetown's national championship team as a senior in 1984, taking away some of the bad taste in his mouth from '83. He took his role as a goat philosophically.

"This is part of growing up," he said.

So it was also for Webber in 1993. The 6-foot-10 Webber was part of the flashy all-freshman "Fab Five" with their aggressive athletic style, black sox, and baggy shorts. The Fab Five created a new college basketball culture and captured the country's imagination.

Webber, joined by Jalen Rose, Ray Jackson, Jimmy King, and Juwan Howard, was most prominent of the five. He was a national high school basketball player of the year who led his Detroit Country Day team to three state championships in Michigan.

The Fab Five all started at Michigan in the fall of 1991 and grew together as a high-flying unit. The notoriety followed them right through the NCAA playoffs, where they advanced to the championship game against North Carolina.

Like the Georgetown game, this one was down to the wire and also involved a mental error.

The Wolverines trailed the Tar Heels 73-71 with 11 seconds remaining in the national championship game. Webber furiously dribbled downcourt, heading for the area near the Michigan bench.

Suddenly, he was trapped at the sideline by two Tar Heels players, George Lynch and Derrick Phelps. They were all over Webber, who had basically painted himself into a corner.

Webber was having trouble finding an open man.

Players on the nearby Wolverines bench were screaming. The crowd was screaming.

What to do?

Webber signaled timeout.

He would have liked to have had that one back.

"It was the heat of the moment," said Wolverines forward Ray Jackson, "Everybody's yelling. You get nervous. He's a 20-year-old kid."

Webber had forgotten that the Wolverines were out of timeouts.

Technical foul!

The referee gave two free throws to Carolina. The Tar Heels finished with two more to clinch a 77-71 victory.

A dazed Webber weaved unsteadily through the crowd that had charged on to the court.

"I don't remember," Webber said of the final seconds at the Superdome. "Just called a timeout, and we didn't have a timeout. And I cost our team the game."

Things were only going to get worse for Webber in the succeeding seasons. He was involved in a play-for-pay scandal, allegedly accepting $200,000 from a school booster and then lying about it to a grand jury. That led to the removal of the two Final Four banners at Crisler Arena, along with the removal of all the wins in '92 and '93 from the record books, and the loss of scholarships. In addition, Webber was forbidden to have any formal contact with the school for 20 years.

Webber left Michigan early to join the NBA, where he had a distinguished career. He left behind a college basketball program in shambles, the Fab Five just a bitter memory.

"He was the person eventually that ended up having the unfortunate timeout," Rose said.

CATCHING A THIEF

This is the story about Babe Ruth's most embarrassing moment on a ball field.

It was Game 7 of the 1926 World Series and the St. Louis Cardinals were three outs away from winning it all. They led the New York Yankees 3-2 with Grover Cleveland Alexander on the mound for the Cards.

Alexander, who pitched a complete game the day before, got the first two batters out in the ninth.

Alexander worked a 3-2 count on the Babe before barely missing the plate on the next pitch. Ruth trotted to first, his fourth walk of the game.

Bob Meusel stepped to the plate as Ruth edged off first. Then Ruth did the unthinkable. Defying all baseball logic, he tried to steal second base.

Cardinals catcher Bob O'Farrell fired to second, where shortstop Honus Wagner was waiting to make the tag.

Game over! World Series over! Cardinals win!!

Ruth later said he had attempted the steal because no one would expect it. Yes, but he didn't count on the picture-perfect throw by O'Farrell, the National League MVP that year.

Surprising as it was, not much was mentioned in the newspaper coverage of the game. However, writer H. I. Phillips of the *Philadelphia Inquirer* did make one cynical remark of Ruth's error in judgment: "It was the case of a behemoth thinking itself a gazelle."

THE LONG AND SHORT OF IT

It was called the "golden age" of sports and few athletes personified the 1920s more than boxer Jack Dempsey. A Dempsey fight usually drew a large gate and national attention.

A rising folk hero since taking the heavyweight championship away from Jess Willard in 1919, the highly popular "Manassa Mauler" from Manassa, Colorado, was known as the people's champion.

Dempsey was renowned for his boxing skills and raw punching power—he had taken apart the mountainous Willard in three savage rounds.

Seven years later Dempsey met his equal in Gene Tunney, a tough ex-Marine. The two would become part of one of the most famous fights in boxing history. Also one of the most controversial.

When they first met in 1926, Tunney outboxed Dempsey in 10 rounds to become the 10th heavyweight champion of the world. In 1927, Dempsey was back in the ring with Tunney hoping to regain his title.

When the two stepped through the ropes at Chicago's Soldier Field, there were more than 100,000 people in the huge stadium. They didn't seem to mind a steady rain, paying a gate of $2.6 million, the highest in boxing history at that point. The crowd included movie stars, giants from the business world, and the governors of nine states. In addition, some 40 to 50 million listened to the bout on national radio.

As the two boxers faced each other in the center of the ring, referee Dave Barry said:

"Now I want to get this point clear, in the event of a knockdown, the man scoring the knockdown will go to the farthest neutral corner."

Both champ and challenger nodded.

In the seventh round, Dempsey connected with a bunch of brutal blows.

"There were several crushing blows, Dempsey battering me with lefts and rights," Tunney later recalled.

Tunney fell against the ropes, collapsing to a sitting position on the canvas. Dempsey refused to move.

"I couldn't move," Dempsey said. "I just couldn't. I wanted him to get up. I wanted to kill [him]."

Barry finally pulled Dempsey away to a neutral corner. By then timekeeper Paul Beeler had started his count and was up to five, expecting Barry to take care of the rest.

But instead of picking up the count at that point, Barry started all over with "one."

The first number that Tunney heard was, "two."

"What a surprise," Tunney recalled. "I had seven seconds in which to get up."

Tunney took almost the full count of 10. Then springing up, Tunney stayed on his feet the rest of the round. In the eighth, Tunney was refreshed enough to finish off Dempsey and retain his championship.

By most conservative estimates, the knockout count was at least 14 seconds. Dempsey's failure to move to a neutral corner had given Tunney extra time to clear his head and cost Dempsey the title.

Dempsey became the goat and the "Long Count" fight became a part of boxing history.

PULLING A FAST ONE

It was the 1957 Kentucky Derby. Willie Shoemaker, atop Gallant Man, was comfortably in front of the field as the horses headed into the homestretch.

So comfortable, in fact, that he misjudged the finish line and eased up on the reins. Shoemaker was overtaken by archrival Bill Hartack atop Iron Liege.

Sports writers tried to find Shoemaker after the race to hear his side of the story. But he had already left the track and was reportedly on his way to the airport for a flight to Los Angeles.

"Yeah, and he'll probably get off at Albuquerque," one of the skeptical sports writers cracked.

HAVING A STROKE

"What a stupid I am."

Roberto De Vicenzo had every right to feel that way after making a huge scorecard mistake at the 1968 Masters.

De Vicenzo had just finished the par-4 17th hole at the world-famous Augusta National Golf Club in Augusta, Georgia. Tommy Aaron was keeping score for De Vicenzo and recorded a par for the Argentine golfer, which De Vicenzo approved.

Wrong. Actually it was one stroke less, a birdie 3.

De Vicenzo went on to officially finish 11 under par, losing the tournament by one stroke to Bob Goalby, 278 to 277. According to the rules, a golfer is disqualified if he signs an incorrect-lower-scorecard. He is allowed to keep the score if a higher number is approved.

De Vicenzo was heartbroken. He would never again challenge for the Masters championship.

"Every now and then I will drop a tear," said De Vicenzo, whose only major victory was the Open championship in 1967, "but I've moved on."

3

SPORTS' GREATEST SCANDALS

The Steroid Era. The Black Sox. Point-shaving. Bounty hunting. The Penn State tragedy.

And that's only the beginning to probing the dark side of Crazyball.

Sports does a lot of good in our lives. But there have always been more sports scandals than you can shake a bat at.

One could argue that sports, with its mutual rooting interest, has done more to promote racial harmony than anything else in America. Fans bond for a singular purpose, relating their lives to famous sports events.

But then there's the other side, the infamous events that somehow are so compelling to fans.

Start with the Steroid Era in baseball, which infected an entire nation and sport and brought down some of the greatest athletes in history.

Is baseball currently on the sick list? Let's see.

THE STEROID ERA

Baseball commissioner Bud Selig would simply like to see it go away. Not so fast.

With a host of players caught in lies or misrepresenting themselves, many of the game's stars continue to fade and lose credibility.

Hardly a day goes by when references aren't made to drug use by players in the major leagues. Or worse, suspensions are meted out.

Hardly a day when a big name isn't connected to it in some way.

Longtime all-star Alex Rodriguez, and Ryan Braun, the American League's Most Valuable Player in 2012, were among the latest to be caught in the ever-widening steroid web.

Such superstars as home run king Barry Bonds, seven-time Cy Young winner Roger Clemens, and popular power hitter Sammy Sosa were all connected to steroid use. Ordinarily surefire candidates for the Baseball Hall of Fame, in 2013, the first vote by the Baseball Writers Association of America (BBWAA) following the Steroid Era, Clemens, Bonds, and Sosa were rejected by the writers. In fact, everyone else was, too.

All 37 players on the ballot, even those who had not been tainted by reports of steroid use, were shut out. Sadly, Cooperstown was quiet for a change. It was the first time since 1996 that no player was voted into the Hall, and only the eighth time overall.

In order to gain entry into the Hall, players must receive at least 75 percent of the votes from the BBWAA. The writers' message was clear: They listed Clemens on only 37.6 percent of the ballots, Bonds on 36.2 and Sosa, who hit over 600 homers, only received 12.5 percent.

Why?

The end of their baseball careers got messy. Bonds, who hit 762 home runs in a spectacular career, faced perjury charges for lying to a grand jury investigating performance-enhancing drug use. After several years of legal entanglements, the seven-time MVP managed to stay out of prison. Bonds got off with what some thought was a slap on the wrist: two years' probation, 250 hours of community service in youth-related activities, and a $4,000 fine.

Clemens, meanwhile, appeared before a now-famous 2008 congressional hearing during which the pitcher vehemently denied usage of steroids.

"Let me be clear: I have never used steroids or HGH," Clemens said arrogantly, throwing a high hard one at the congressmen.

Like Bonds, Clemens faced perjury charges for lying to a grand jury. But Clemens had to face them twice. His first court appearance ended in a mistrial and Clemens headed back for a retrial, in which he was found not guilty of lying to Congress about steroids and human growth hormone.

Brian McNamee, Clemens's strength coach, was the government's key witness, allegedly the one who introduced Clemens to steroids. And to prove it, he said, he kept the needles. Clemens's lawyers, meanwhile, tried to discredit McNamee. They claimed that McNamee had a past that "contains more dirt than a pitcher's mound."

Sosa, meanwhile, faded into the background upon leaving baseball, the goodwill he once engendered in his rivalry with

Mark McGwire now largely forgotten. The two sluggers, who staged the greatest home run race since Roger Maris and Mickey Mantle to revive the game following a players' strike and World Series cancellation in 1994, both had their careers tainted by steroids accusations.

Selig, meanwhile, hoped that long-term suspensions for steroid use would be enough to help keep the game clean. He's still crossing his fingers.

THE BLACK SOX SCANDAL

"Say it ain't so, Joe."

A teary-eyed boy had pushed to the front of the line to confront "Shoeless" Joe Jackson.

According to some accounts, Jackson had just left a courthouse in Chicago in 1921 when he was stopped by an incredulous young fan who was seeking the truth.

Jackson and seven of his Chicago White Sox teammates were accused of accepting bribes from gamblers to throw the 1919 World Series. The heavily favored White Sox lost the Series that year to the underdog Cincinnati Reds, five games to three in a time when the Series was decided in nine games instead of the current seven.

Although the eight players were acquitted in a court of law, they were nevertheless banned from the game for life by Kenesaw Mountain Landis, the hard-hitting commissioner brought in by team owners to clean up baseball. He did, in a big way, his attention mainly focused on the case that would forever be known as the "Black Sox Scandal."

Jackson, the colorful ballplayer nicknamed "Shoeless Joe," was the highest-profile player in the group. Jackson would leave the game with the third highest batting average in baseball history, .356, one season hitting a remarkable, still-standing rookie record of .408.

In the 1919 World Series, Jackson hardly looked like anyone trying to throw a Series. He hit .375, knocked in six runs, scored five, and handled 16 chances in the field without an error. That did not let Jackson off the hook, and baseball's Hall of Fame doors were shut to him and his seven teammates forever.

Jackson's implicated teammates: Eddie Cicotte, Oscar "Happy" Felsch, Arnold "Chick" Gandil, Fred McMullin, Charles "Swede" Risberg, George "Buck" Weaver, and Claude "Lefty" Williams.

By most accounts, it was Gandil's relationship with gamblers that sparked the fix. According to Gandil, it was a common practice in those days to fix games for gambling purposes. Hall of Famers Ty Cobb and Tris Speaker were allegedly involved in such activities.

"Ballplayers all mixed with gamblers in those days," Gandil admitted in an interview many years after the Black Sox scandal.

But Gandil steadfastly refused to have any association with fixing the 1919 Series. "I never confessed," he said.

Too young to retire from the game he loved, Jackson continued to play in various levels of baseball outside the majors, and usually under an assumed name. All the while he proclaimed his innocence in the Black Sox scandal until his death at the age of 51.

An illiterate son of a South Carolina millworker, Jackson acquired his "Shoeless Joe" nickname while playing in his home town of Greenville, South Carolina, in 1908. The outfielder had asked to sit out one game because his new shoes were giving him blisters. But the team was shorthanded, and Jackson was forced to play. He tossed off his spikes and played, hitting a triple in his bare feet.

As Jackson surged into third base, one of the fans yelled, "You shoeless son of a gun, you!"

The nickname stuck. It's just not found anywhere in Cooperstown.

SAY IT AIN'T SO, PETE

"I would have been better off using steroids, being an alcoholic, doing drugs, or being a spouse abuser. All those guys get second chances, but not me."

Pete Rose, baseball's all-time hits king, was bemoaning his plight. It was 2011 and Rose, persona non grata in baseball since 1989, was making his case for a return to his beloved sport. Maybe even a place in the Hall of Fame.

So far, he was striking out.

Rose was banned for life for gambling activities after an investigation by Major League Baseball. Bart Giamatti, the commissioner who banned Rose, died one week after that decision. As of 2013, nothing had changed in the commissioner's office regarding Rose.

"I have to do what I think is right, like the eight who preceded me did what they thought was right," said baseball commissioner Bud Selig about Rose's case. "I've done what I think is right."

That is, keep Rose out of baseball.

Ballplayers and gambling are nothing new in baseball, of course. Along with the 1919 Black Sox, such high-profile players as Ty Cobb and Tris Speaker, both Hall of Famers, were allegedly involved in gambling activities in the 1920s. They were forced by Commissioner Landis to resign managerial positions before they were allowed to come back to baseball. Unlike Rose, they did come back.

Hall of Famers "aren't all altar guys," Rose says.

Rose, meanwhile, continued to campaign for his place in the Hall. Judged on accomplishments alone, he would already be there. Rose's 4,256 hits were more than anyone's in baseball history. Most of them were accumulated during a fabulous career with the Cincinnati Reds when he was known as "Charlie Hustle" because of his hard-driving style of play.

Whether a meaningless All-Star Game or the World Series, Rose played the game with equal abandon. Hey, he ran to first base on ball four.

Baseball fans may recall Rose's hard slide into home in the 1970 All-Star Game that injured American League catcher Ray Fosse and impacted the rest of Fosse's career.

Rose played for the Philadelphia Phillies and Montreal Expos and returned to Cincinnati before retiring to manage the Reds from 1984–1989, when Giamatti kicked him out of baseball. Rose had other problems: He spent five months in jail for tax evasion in 1990.

It took Rose 15 years to acknowledge that he had gambled while he was managing the Reds. Finally in 2004, he made the admission: Yes, he had bet on baseball games. And he apologized.

In the meantime, Rose continued on a singular path, signing autographs at baseball shows and marketing himself on TV. Anything to make a buck.

"I know guys like Mays, Aaron, Yastrzemski wouldn't do this," Rose told *Sports Illustrated.* "But it feels natural to me."

Just like hitting a baseball.

LITTLE LEAGUE, BIG LIE

In the 2001 Little League season, one particular youngster was pitching a brilliant game, shutting down batters with his fastball, curve, and changeup.

He looked almost too good for a 12-year-old.

He was.

Danny Almonte was 14 years old, overage for Little League play. He was living the Big Lie.

One day he was the star of one of the best Little League teams in America. The overpowering lefthander had thrown the first perfect game in the Little Leagues in 44 years. He won all four games he pitched for the Rolando Paulino All-Stars of the Bronx, giving up only one unearned run and three hits, striking out 62 of 72 batters.

He was a national celebrity, receiving phone calls from big-league stars. He was a media darling.

The next thing you knew, he and his father were outcasts, the father and son banned from Little League baseball forever.

It all came unraveled when Felipe de Jesus Almonte lied about his son's age.

Like many other kids in the Dominican Republic, Danny Almonte played baseball as soon as he could walk. And like many other fathers in the Dominican Republic, Felipe Almonte had a dream: someday his son would play in the major leagues.

For years the Caribbean region has turned out excellent baseball talent from Puerto Rico, the Dominican Republic, and Cuba, among others. There was opportunity for Danny Almonte. Felipe Almonte set a course for his son.

Danny's love of baseball came from his father, who established a youth league in the Dominican Republic.

"When he was a little boy, he always walked around with a little stick, hitting things, batting," said his mother, Sonia Margarita Rojas Breton.

Felipe made his way to New York after a divorce. He reportedly brought his son to the United States in June 2000 on a 12-month tourist visa.

One of the papers that Felipe prized: Danny's birth certificate. Born April 7, 1989, it said. Proof positive, he said.

It would later come into question through an investigative story by a national magazine. But first there was the Little League and a loss in the 2000 Eastern Regional final.

The following year, Danny Almonte was the star. He blew away hitters with a fastball that equated to 90 mph in the majors; the Little League mound was closer to home plate.

With his command of pitches and presence on the mound with the Paulino All-Stars, Almonte appeared to be a good deal older than many of the other players. That created suspicion among teams that Paulino, a sports writer who founded the All-Stars, was using players older than 12.

The Paulino team manager, Alberto Gonzalez, disputed those claims.

"He's just a little more mature right now," Gonzalez said.

There was no evidence that Almonte was any older than 12, the required age maximum for Little League ball. One of the teams hired detectives to investigate, but they found no evidence of wrongdoing.

When the questions kept coming, the Little League director of media relationships, Lance Van Auken, pulled out the birth certificate dated April 7, 1989. On the back were red and green stamps of authenticity.

How had the fraud been perpetrated?

A *Sports Illustrated* reporter dug up a copy of Danny Almonte's real birth certificate, dated two years earlier in 1987. That officially made him 14.

All birth records in the Dominican Republic are recorded in two places: the central office in Santo Domingo and the local office in Moca. In the central office, on March 21, 2000, Felipe registered the boy's birth for the second time. This time, he took two years off Danny's birthdate.

A scandal erupted, drawing not only international attention but also a response from the White House. President George W. Bush's administration asked the Dominican government to investigate. Records experts determined that the birth certificate was falsified and that Danny Almonte, whose team reached the World Series before elimination, was actually 14.

The Little League turned the issue into a positive lesson. As a result of the scandal, stricter guidelines were instituted in determining the age of players. The Little League now requires not only a birth certificate, but three proofs of residences, and local league officials must sign an affidavit affirming they have seen the copy of the birth certificate. If the teams advance, the documents are checked again.

"We're a better program today because of it," said Little League president Stephen Keener.

WHO WAS THAT LADY?

"You're number one! You're number one!" People shouted encouragement as Jacqueline Gareau passed by along the crowded, noisy streets of Boston.

Gareau was finishing her run in the 1980 Boston Marathon in the time of 2:34.28. Elated, sweaty, and exhausted, Gareau crossed the finish line. She had trained three years for the Boston run. Now it was paying off for the massage therapist from Quebec.

She was escorted to the interview tent to meet the press.

But who was that lady wearing the winner's laurel wreath? She had seemed to materialize out of nowhere. She had crossed the finish line three minutes before Gareau.

"Who is she?" Gareau asked.

"She won," she was told.

"But people along the route, they told me I was number one. The first woman."

To say Gareau was surprised was an understatement. Shocked would be more like it.

How could it be?

The woman who finished three minutes ahead of her didn't look anything like a runner just completing a 26-mile race. She wasn't sweaty, hair matted down and body exhausted.

Thus began an infamous incident in America's most famous marathon race: Rosie Ruiz's make-believe Boston run.

The 26-year-old, Cuban-born Ruiz was an enigmatic figure as she crossed the finish line ahead of 448 women in the Boston race on April 21, 1980. Within minutes Rosie's claim to fame was questioned.

Her heart rate was questioned. Her appearance lacked the sweat and signs of a marathoner who had just run 26-plus miles. She couldn't remember any details of the course. She was unfamiliar with terms such as splits, which runners use as a way of measuring their pace.

The event's officials had a problem: How to prove she was a fraud?

The event was not televised and officials scrambled to find evidence to support or deny.

The Marathon photos showed no Rosie.

The checkpoints for her number 50? Never registered.

And perhaps the most damning evidence of all—nobody remembered seeing her until the end of the race.

Yet Rosie insisted she won!

"I knew something was fishy," said four-time Boston Marathon winner Bill Rodgers after Ruiz had clocked the third-best women's time in race history at 2:31.56.

Ruiz had not much experience in long-distance running, hardly any at all, in fact.

Only six months before, Ruiz had participated in the New York Marathon under questionable circumstances. A photographer spotted Ruiz on a subway the day of the race. Ruiz told her she had injured her ankle. She was on her way to the finish line to inform officials that she was hurt.

Ruiz was erroneously given an official certificate stating she had finished the New York race. She received the needed qualifying time for the Boston race.

It would be easy, wouldn't it? One theory: Ruiz could use the crowd as a screen, then pop out at an opportune moment to finish the race.

Did Rosie expect to be the victor? Perhaps not. But she stuck to her story as the winner of the women's Boston Marathon.

She was stripped of her title eight days later.

She never entered the Boston Marathon after that. There is no record of Ruiz ever competing in another marathon. However, Gareau is a veteran with nine victories in various marathons to her credit.

"I always say that the most famous marathoner of all time is Rosie Ruiz," Rodgers said. "I guess infamous is more accurate."

BLOWING THE WHISTLE

It was the greatest point-shaving scandal in college basketball history. And it started where the money was, New York's Madison Square Garden, a gamblers' paradise.

It didn't only happen in New York, but was widespread, all over a good portion of the country. It was 1951 and college basketball players were learning how to cheat.

Manhattan basketball coach Ken Norton was aware of isolated cases of point-shaving in the city, most notably at Brooklyn College. There were rumors that fixing games was now more extensive.

Norton didn't believe that his team would be infected by such activity.

"In those days, there were a lot of rumors that there was a possibility that the college lads were involved in leveling games, to favor the gamblers," Norton said. "But with the quality of the other schools in New York like CCNY, NYU, and St. John's, I didn't figure we could be involved. We were low man on the totem pole."

That was about to change.

On January 11, 1951, just before the Jaspers were to leave for a game in Jersey City against St. Peter's, Manhattan's star center Junius Kellogg approached Norton. He told the Manhattan coach he had just been offered $1,000 to make sure the Jaspers lose to DePaul the following week at Madison Square Garden.

Making the offer was none other than Hank Poppe, cocaptain of the previous year's team and the second-leading scorer in Manhattan basketball history. Poppe had established a classic pattern: He offered players money to either lose games or keep the point spread at a specific limit to favor the gamblers' bets. This was called "leveling games" or "point-shaving." Gamblers bet heavily on the games, knowing which team would lose or what area the point spread would be in.

"Writers had been telling me about this stuff for a long time," Norton said. "But I never had the proof until Kellogg came to me one day and told me that he had been offered a thousand dollars to see that we lose the DePaul game."

This is the way the conversation went between Kellogg and Norton:

"He said I could get rich."

"Really?"

"For just missing a few baskets, throwing a bad pass or two, slowing down a bit . . ."

"A thousand dollars for that?"

"We have to lose by more than the point spread."

Kellogg was shocked. Poppe was one of the Jaspers' all-time greats. Kellogg had admired him. Now Kellogg was the Jaspers' big star, and the one player on the team most in position to control the flow of a game.

When Kellogg was growing up in Rocky Mount, North Carolina, the eldest of 11 children, money was scarce. But one could not deny Kellogg's basketball talent. It was rich and plentiful. He used that skill to leap from the backwoods of North Carolina to the front sports pages in New York City.

"Just keep your mouth shut and go," Norton told Kellogg. "I'll take care of it."

Norton's sleep was less than peaceful that night. With Kellogg's striking testimony still burning in his ears, he had taken the Jaspers to Jersey City to play St. Peter's. Meanwhile, he had set up an appointment to see the president of Manhattan College, Brother Bonaventure Thomas.

Still ahead was a televised game with Temple in Philadelphia on Saturday before the Jaspers were to face DePaul at the Garden on Tuesday night. The Jaspers won the Temple game—although Norton wasn't sure how.

"I really had a tough time thinking about Temple with this gambling stuff on my mind," Norton said. "It wasn't an easy thing to keep on your mind. I had to keep it under wraps. I couldn't tell anyone, not even my wife. It was too big."

He did, however, tell authorities. Thus began the greatest point-shaving scandal in college basketball history.

Kellogg's role in the affair would be significant. In a period of six days, from the time Kellogg was approached by Poppe to fix a basketball game in Madison Square Garden, and the apprehension of gamblers at a midtown bar, an incredible cloak-and-dagger story unfolded that matched any detective tale of its time. During that nerve-racking week, Kellogg played the role of an undercover agent and Norton his counselor and confidant.

Kellogg was told to play along with the gamblers. Authorities were setting up the trap. So when Poppe called on Sunday to follow up on his offer to Kellogg, the player really sounded interested.

They set up a meeting.

"He took me to a saloon on Broadway, and we had some beers," Kellogg said of Poppe. "He told me about other people in the setup, former players. Jack Byrnes, for one." (Byrnes was co-captain with Poppe the previous year.)

Poppe said the fix was still on for Tuesday night at the Garden. Poppe said he would see Kellogg at courtside and tell him what the betting spread would be.

Oh, yes, one more thing:

"He also said it was worth my life to keep my mouth shut about it," Kellogg said.

Kellogg had wrestled with that notion, of course, ever since Poppe had first contacted him. When you do business with gamblers, there was always that danger. But how could he face himself if he didn't do all he could to expose the gamblers? His life wouldn't be worth much anyway if he didn't stick to his principles.

The noose was tightening around the gamblers.

"Be at the arena early Tuesday," Norton told Kellogg.

The Manhattan-DePaul game was part of a college doubleheader that night.

"We were playing the first game," Norton recalled, "and it was an important game, too. Both of us were undefeated. Our plan was then to wire Kellogg for sound."

Just about every gambler in town apparently heard the fix was on and bet heavily against Manhattan.

"Never in my life did I see such one-way action," one bookie said. "Everybody wanted to get something down on DePaul. Kids who never bet more than $10 in their life wanted to get down for $300. They were betting for the wise guys."

Wiring and all, Kellogg shot practice baskets with the rest of the Manhattan team. As expected, Poppe approached Kellogg at courtside.

"Thirteen points," Poppe whispered to Kellogg, meaning that the Jaspers had to lose by at least 13 points to DePaul.

Poppe added instructions:

"On the rebounds, miss the ball occasionally or throw hook shots over the basket. After the rebounds, don't pass as fast. That might save two points. Don't try to block the other guy's shot. And whatever you do, don't stink up the joint."

Poppe was unaware that his every move was being watched. It seemed that every detective in New York was at the game.

Norton: "The team came back into the dressing room and I grabbed Kellogg by the arm and pulled him out of the ranks and he's telling me, 'Thirteen points.' I tried to keep him quiet."

Kellogg's brief talk with Poppe had made his heart jump. The significance of the conversation inflamed Kellogg's whole being, and his nervousness was apparent from the opening tap. He missed his first two shots by such wide margins that Norton thought, "He looks like he's actually dumping the game, he's so damn tight. He's trying like hell and nothing can go right for the kid. I'm telling you, he's missing hangers in there."

Norton sent in a replacement, Charlie Genering. Kellogg walked to courtside and hit the Manhattan bench with a resounding "plop." He mopped his face with a towel and sighed heavily.

"Take it easy, kid," Norton told Kellogg, patting his knee.

Kellogg quietly contemplated his sneakers, but each roar from the Garden crowd told him that his teammates were doing well.

Genering had especially played well in Kellogg's place, hitting his first eight shots. He had 17 points by the half to help the Jaspers take a 37-28 lead. Kellogg, playing intermittently, had scored a substandard six points and picked up only two rebounds.

Genering continued to play well after intermission. With his teammates complementing his game, Manhattan's "sure losers" beat DePaul 62-59.

There was a prearranged meeting set up between Kellogg and Poppe. But Poppe was unable to keep the date.

He was picked up by detectives and quickly confessed to misdeeds. He told authorities not only about his bribe attempts, but also about games he had fixed as a player. He and Byrnes, as co-captain of the 1949-50 team, had received weekly retainers of $40 each from the gamblers. For three Manhattan defeats (against Bradley, Santa Clara, and Siena), they had received $1,000 after each game. They also received cash for controlling the point spread in two other games.

The arrest of Poppe and his cohorts on the night of January 16, 1951, was the first big break in the point-shaving investigations for detectives who had been chasing nothing but shadows for years.

Suddenly, everything fell into place for the authorities. Coaches who felt no gamblers could touch their kids were shocked. And college basketball was about to be ripped apart as repercussions went nationwide.

Gamblers had reached stars of Adolph Rupp's Kentucky team that won two successive NCAA championships. CCNY players who won the double championship of the NCAA and NIT were caught cheating. And eight players from Bradley, runner-up to CCNY in both title games, played ball with the gamblers.

There seemed to be no end of teams affected because it reached from the East Coast to the Midwest and the South. All told, 32 players from seven schools were implicated in fixing 87 games from 1947–1951.

Another major point-shaving scandal followed in the early 1960s that involved 32 schools. Although this one was much larger than the first, the scandal of '51 was considered the Big One because it represented the first major breakthrough in the point-shaving investigations. And it took the courage of one player from New York to bring down the gamblers.

"They picked Kellogg because he was black and underprivileged and therefore he would go for it," Norton said. "But they just picked the wrong kid."

ROGUE REFEREE

NBA referee Tim Donaghy had a problem. His gambling debts were getting higher and higher.

There was an easy solution for an unscrupulous referee who had access to valuable information that gamblers could use. And it was worth money. Lots of money.

During the 2006–07 season, Donaghy admitted to federal investigators that he had communicated information to gamblers. He was paid well and continued to do so until he was implicated in an FBI investigation.

Knowing before tip-off which referees are working the game is valuable information for gamblers. It was this kind of information that Donaghy provided.

Donaghy pleaded guilty to felony charges of taking cash payoffs from gamblers during the 2006-07 season. He confessed to betting on games and passing on information to gamblers.

NBA commissioner David Stern called Donaghy a "rogue, isolated criminal" operating on his own, without cooperation from any other referee. On a radio show Stern said that the scandal was a "wakeup call. It says you can't be complacent."

An investigation ensued by the NBA. No other referees were implicated.

Convicted, Donaghy spent 15 months in prison.

When Donaghy got out of prison, he received $1.5 million for his tell-all book. In a quirky turnabout, Donaghy began evaluating referees' calls for a website during big games.

You can't make this stuff up.

FOOTBALL FOLLIES

There was a new sheriff in town.

With guns blazing, Roger Goodell took over as NFL commissioner in 2006.

Criminal activity? Not tolerated under Goodell's new Player Conduct Policy. Goodell had taken over for Paul Tagliabue and, make no mistake, he was in charge.

Spygate? Bountygate? Goodell said he would do whatever it took to protect the integrity of the game, of the "NFL Shield."

Spygate was the talk of the NFL in 2007 after the staff of New England Patriots coach Bill Belichick was caught videotaping the New York Jets' sideline signals during a game.

Belichick didn't consider it cheating. After the tapes were reviewed, Goodell had them destroyed to prevent leaks.

The sheriff came down hard on the Patriots:

Coach fined $500,000.

Team fined $250,000.

The loss of a first-round draft pick.

Few of the thorny issues that Goodell faced compared to the bounty-hunting controversy in 2012. The story mostly centered on the New Orleans Saints.

Under a system created by New Orleans coaches and players, each Saint was offered cash to deliberately attempt to injure opponents. The media called it "Bountygate."

According to the NFL, 22 to 27 defensive players, as well as defensive coordinator Gregg Williams, maintained the "bounty" payments over three seasons, 2009-11.

Under the program, such terms as "cart-offs" and "knockouts" became common expressions. When an opponent was removed on a stretcher or a cart, it was called a cart-off and earned the player who made the hit $1,000. When an opponent couldn't come back for the rest of the game, it was called a knockout. That was worth $1,500.

There was also cash for legitimate hits.

"The payments here are particularly troubling because they involve not just payments for performance, but also for injuring opposition players," said Goodell, who was in the center of a movement to enhance player safety when this scandal hit.

Concussions have always been a problem in a violent sport like football. A group of former players sued the NFL claiming they were not given enough protection when they played, nor warned of the dangers of the sport. Goodell was determined to give present-day players better conditions. He would send a message to any individual team that even considered using a bounty system.

When the NFL closed the case on the Saints, head coach Sean Payton was suspended for a year. It was the first time in NFL history that a coach was suspended for any reason. While Payton did not participate in the program, he was aware of it and failed to stop it.

Williams was also barred indefinitely—he returned to the NFL in 2013 with the Tennessee Titans—and four players in leadership positions, including linebacker Jonathan Vilma, were suspended. They were later reinstated after appeals.

The sheriff was still on the job.

UNHAPPY VALLEY

Who would have believed it?

A legendary football coach, revered by just about everyone.

A pristine program, the envy of the college football world.

Penn State University, an educational institution top in its class.

Happy Valley—until the ugliest of scandals tore through central Pennsylvania in 2011.

The football program at Penn State was faced with an unenviable climb out of the depths. The student body had to come to grips with the unspeakable.

One man, Jerry Sandusky, shattered the pristine Penn State image, brought it tumbling down with shocking swiftness, spiraling it down in shambles. A pedophile among innocents.

How crazy was the Sandusky scandal at Penn State?

Crazy enough so that all that remained was a shattered legacy for Joe Paterno. His famed statue no longer stands on guard at Beaver Stadium, stolen away in the night.

Some feel sanctions by the NCAA were unfair: penalizing the coach and the school. Taking away games that the Nittany Lions had won under Paterno, games and championships—111 victories in all from 1998–2011. A loss of scholarships, no bowl games for five years, and a $60 million fine.

Others feel they weren't stringent enough.

Despite such sanctions, and the loss of several key players, the Lions went 8-4 in the 2012 season under Bill O'Brien, the first fulltime head coach other than Paterno in nearly half a century.

First down and a long way to go.

4

CRAZY PRANKS, SILLY STUNTS

JACK, LEE, AND THE SNAKE

Jack Nicklaus owned eight major pro golf championships when he approached the first tee for an 18-hole playoff with Lee Trevino in 1971 at storied Merion Golf Club in Ardmore, Pennsylvania. He was all business and sat down under a tree for some shade before Trevino appeared.

Then Trevino showed the world why he was the self-proclaimed "Merry Mex." And his loosey-goosey approach helped Trevino win that playoff against the man many consider the greatest golfer ever.

Playing to the gallery, Trevino waved, then dug deep into the side pocket of his golf bag. Instead of grabbing a special golf ball for the round, he pulled out a three-foot-long rubber snake.

The stunned crowd squealed as Trevino, almost convulsed in laughter, tossed the toy at Nicklaus, who danced out of the way. He, too, was hysterical.

"I need all the help I can get," Trevino said as the tension of the big event melted away.

Then Trevino beat Nicklaus 68-71 to win his second U.S. Open on the way to eight major titles.

Nicklaus would recover to win a record 18 majors.

FAN MAN

The second heavyweight championship fight between Riddick Bowe and Evander Holyfield was as hyped as boxing matches can get. When both stepped into the outdoor ring at Caesars Palace in Las Vegas on November 6, 1993, they had no clue that an interloper from the heavens would steal their thunder.

During the seventh round of a pretty good fight, James Miller, the self-proclaimed "Fan Man," crashed his motorized paraglider into the ring ropes. He was seeking publicity, of course, but the first thing he got was a big-time beating from the folks manning Bowe's corner.

Miller was taken away by security after giving Bowe, the champion, a bigger scare than Holyfield had been doing. Bowe's pregnant wife, Judy, fainted. One of Bowe's aides, Bernard Brooks Sr., needed stitches from a cut on the head after Miller's device struck him.

Among those in the crowd were the Rev. Jesse Jackson, who helped tend to Judy Bowe, and Louis Farrakhan of the Nation of Islam.

Miller was charged only with a misdemeanor dangerous flying violation and released on $200 bail a few hours after the incident.

"I can't believe they didn't find something more serious to charge this guy with," promoter Dan Duva said. "If he had landed a couple of rows earlier, he could have killed somebody. He could have killed Riddick's wife. And if he didn't get caught up in the lights, he could have come right inside the ring and hurt the fighters."

As Tim Dahlberg of The Associated Press wrote: "It was the perfect stage for the ultimate outrageous stunt."

But Miller never got the fame he sought, even if his act remains near the top of sports stunt infamy.

PENNIES FROM RUSTY

Late in a 1997 race at Martinsville Speedway, Hall of Fame driver Rusty Wallace was in front during a restart. But NASCAR black-flagged him for jumping the restart, and Wallace didn't win.

Ticked off, Wallace was asked by a radio reporter how he felt, and he cursed.

"Not only did I lose the race but was fined $5,000 for saying an expletive on the radio," Wallace told *Circle Track Magazine*. "That really got me hot."

So hot that Wallace decided to pay the fine in pennies at the next race, which was at Charlotte.

"I called First Union Bank and they put half a million pennies on an armored truck and sent it to the speedway," Wallace said, laughing. "I've never seen so many pennies in my life. I had told [NASCAR president] Bill France what I was going to do and he said he would play my game."

Everyone posed for photos with the sacks of pennies, which gave NASCAR lots of media exposure. Wallace sort of thought the fine would be rescinded.

Instead, "France called me aside and told me to get those damned pennies out of there or he was going to fine me $10,000."

Wallace sent the pennies back to the bank and wrote out a check for $5,000.

OOPS, I DROPPED THE TROPHY

Billy Donovan was not doing the Gator Chomp when he accidentally sent the NCAA championship trophy hurtling to the floor, where it smashed to pieces. He wasn't doing anything accidental at all.

After Florida won its first national title in 2006, Coach Donovan decided to start Midnight Madness—when teams can begin practice for the new season in October—with a crash and a bang.

To loud applause at the arena, Donovan was handed the trophy, held it above his head for the crowd to ogle, then sought to nonchalantly hand it to an assistant. While looking the other way.

The prize plummeted down and broke into hundreds of pieces when it hit the stage floor as star forward Al Horford freaked out.

Then Donovan let everyone in on his little secret: The ruined trophy was a replica. He'd pulled a Friday the 13th prank. The real thing was still intact.

And so was Florida's mini-dynasty as it repeated as national champs in 2007.

EAT UP, LOU

When star outfielder Ken Griffey Jr. lost a bet to Seattle manager Lou Piniella, it was supposed to cost Griffey a steak dinner.

Griffey had a better idea: How about lots of steak dinners for Lou?

After Griffey couldn't back up his bet by hitting home runs to left field, center, and then right on three successive swings during batting practice in spring training 1995, it was time to pay up.

So Griffey had a live cow shipped to Piniella's office in the clubhouse. There's no account of how many steaks Sweet Lou carved out of it.

"WE SUCK"

Harvard vs. Yale always is a huge rivalry, whether on the field, on the courts, in the classrooms, or in business.

Often, fans at Harvard-Yale games are a part of the action, too. In 2004, at aged Harvard Stadium, 20 Yale students took the espionage route at The Game, the annual football duel between the Crimson and the Bulldogs.

The Yalies impersonated the Harvard Pep Squad, which doesn't exist—what, you think Ivy Leaguers are too cool for such stuff?—and handed out white-and-red cards to Harvard fans. Those fans were encouraged to display them in unison and they would read: "GO HARVARD."

The brainiacs from the Cambridge campus, students and alumni alike, some of America's best and brightest, fell for it. When they were told to hold up the cards, ever obedient to Old Crimson, they did it, spelling out "WE SUCK."

Did it matter much? Well, Harvard won in a rout, 35-3, the fourth of five straight wins in the series.

SNAKE RIVER HOAX

Daredevil Evel Knievel never met a challenge he wouldn't take on. And by the time in 1974 he announced he would jump the Snake River Canyon in Idaho on a rocket-powered "Skycycle," he was being paid handsomely for his exploits.

Knievel was getting $6 million for this particular stunt, which was supposed to carry him across the three-quarter-mile canyon safely to the other side. It was to be shown on national TV as the headline attraction of then-iconic ABC anthology *Wide World of Sports*.

Either he was ill-prepared for this jump or he knew exactly what he was doing. After two unmanned practice jumps with his "Skycycle," Knievel went ahead with the jump on, essentially, a jet-powered sled.

He took off from an inclined runway at the edge of the canyon—Knievel oversaw construction of the ramp—and was in the air only a few seconds.

He did clear the edge of the canyon, then his parachute opened. Accidentally and prematurely, Knievel would claim. Others believed it was his, well, golden parachute, considering how much money he was making and how unlikely completing the jump was.

Knievel slowly dropped into the canyon and appeared ready to land in the raging river—not a pleasant thought, because he easily could have drowned. But he landed on the rocks at the edge of the water, dry and safe.

A monument now marks the site of the stunt gone awry.

FOOLISH FUTBOL

The world's most popular sport has had more than its share of wild stunts and pranks. Here are three, two sort of involving soccer's greatest player, Pelé.

The Brazilian star made his debut in the United States with the Cosmos when they played Dallas in a friendly contest at Downing Stadium on Randall's Island. If there has ever been a worse pitch than that venue, where broken glass and garbage often were imbedded in the turf, no one can remember it.

Not even Pelé, who grew up playing barefoot in Brazil with a ball made from a roll of socks.

But the game was being televised by CBS—back in the 1970s, even though soccer had made little impact in the States, huge stars such as Pelé still drew lots of attention; 300 media members were credentialed. So there was no chance of postponement, cancellation, or, even best, instant demolition of Downing.

Instead, Pelé, a winner of three World Cups and perhaps the most famous and beloved athlete on Earth (outside the

USA, of course) was put in danger of injury on a totally unfit pitch.

But the Cosmos got innovative and, without telling many of the players, including Pelé, painted the dirt portion of the field green for the benefit of television. Pelé panicked, telling general manager Clive Toye that he must have some sort of disease because his legs had turned green. He should be scratched from the game.

Instead, Toye told Pelé about the paint job and to not worry; it would wash off. And the Black Pearl then faced off against the Tornado, with the game ending 2-2.

Even thousands of miles from where Pelé might be, he has had an effect, sometimes comical, on a match.

There's the tale of a player in a lower-division English soccer game being knocked unconscious. He was brought to the sideline and revived.

The team's manager asked the trainer, "How is he?" The trainer responded, "He thinks he's in Brazil."

So the quick-thinking manager replied: "Tell him he's Pelé and send him back in."

Not so witty, but certainly a memorable stunt, was pulled off by Chile goalkeeper Roberto Rojas in a 1989 World Cup qualifier at Rio de Janeiro.

Chile was down 1-0 to Brazil when a firecracker exploded not far from Rojas and on the field. He collapsed and while on the ground, used a razor blade he had stashed in his sock to cut his scalp. With blood coming from the wound and smoke all around, Rojas claimed he had been wounded by the explosion.

TV video said otherwise, and after the match was suspended, so was Rojas. An investigation led to FIFA banning him for life.

CUBAN CRISIS

Mavericks owner Mark Cuban's love of basketball might be surpassed only by his hatred for NBA officials. Luckily for Cuban, he has deep pockets as a billionaire. He's emptied plenty of dollars out of them while being fined for criticizing referees.

So when Cuban marched onto the court against New Orleans and got into a shoving match with a ref, well, how long a suspension could Cuban expect? Maybe lifetime?

How about none? Check the calendar date: April 1, 2010.

The ref was no ref at all, and the stunt was orchestrated. As Cuban pushed the official, one of the Mavericks' equipment managers pulled him away before the incident escalated into a full fight.

Several Dallas players were stunned to see their boss getting physical with a ref. Assistant coach Del Harris had no idea what was going on and nearly panicked.

When everyone finally caught on, there were plenty of laughs—even from the real refs.

GRAB THAT MASCOT

Navy's goat and Army's mule are among the most established animal mascots in sports. That has made them living, breathing targets of some covert operations by both military academies.

While Navy has been dominating the football series in recent years, Army has always proven astute at getting the Middies' goat. Literally.

The skullduggery began in 1953, one week before the Army-Navy showdown. Several Cadets infiltrated the Naval Academy, aided by a West Point exchange student living in Annapolis. They found the goat's home near the stadium, stuck him into a car, and headed north to West Point, even, legend has it, with the goat's horns ruining the roof of the convertible.

When the Corps gathered for dinner and a pep rally, the goatnappers presented their prize to the entire cheering Corps before they were ordered to return it to Annapolis.

Even better for the Cadets, they beat Navy 20-7 that year.

That was only the start of the goat-mule pranks. Naval Academy historian Jack Clary once said, "the Navy goat has spent more time on the New Jersey Turnpike than a Greyhound [bus]."

The Cadets once pulled off a goatnapping, then posted an ad in the *New York Times* asking: "Hey Navy! Do you know where your 'kid' is today? The Corps does."

As recently as 2012, Bill the Goat was found attached to a median near the Pentagon. No member of the Corps took credit, though many members of the Corps wore suspiciously wry smiles heading into the game.

But Navy got its vengeance with yet another victory. And the Middies have gotten the upper hand in such pranks, too.

In 1991, with Navy in the midst of a winless season, 17 midshipmen stole onto the U.S. Military Academy campus at

West Point, New York, and stole away with the four Army mules. At the Navy pep rally in Annapolis, the mules were front and center.

The Midshipmen planned for nearly one year, even disguising themselves as tourists when they visited West Point. They saw where the mules were housed, took photographs, and then made diagrams.

"We went up there and said, 'Hey, are these the Army mules?' They told us more than we needed to know," Middie Shawn Callahan said.

Army Major Jim Peterson claimed the Midshipmen messed up with their stunt.

"They have done something to further excite the corps of cadets here at West Point and the Army football team. Unfortunately for Navy, that just means there will be a bigger loss for them when they play tomorrow," he said on the eve of the game.

Surprise: Navy won for the only time all year, 24-3.

5

SICK PLAYS

Really, *REALLY* Awesome Moments

Franco's catch, Flutie's throw, and Bill's blast.

Where were you when Franco Harris made his "Immaculate Reception" to win an NFL playoff game for the Pittsburgh Steelers, Doug Flutie answered a prayer for Boston College with his Hail Mary pass, and Bill Mazeroski hit a home run to win a World Series for the Pittsburgh Pirates?

Topping any of these three spectacular plays would be hard to do. Well, we can try.

Here are some of the sickest plays to make their marks on American sports history:

First, Franco's catch:

"It was being in the right place at the right time, that's all I can really say," Harris said of his legendary moment.

But it was so much more than that.

In the 1972 draft, there had been divided feelings about Harris in the Steelers' front office. Some thought the Steelers should draft Lydell Mitchell, Harris's outstanding backfield mate at Penn State. But Harris became the ultimate choice for the Steelers, drafted in the first round, 13th overall.

Harris hardly made an impression with the Steelers at first.

"He came to camp and kind of tiptoed a little bit," former Steelers safety Mike Wagner said of Harris. "But as the season progressed and you saw some of his moves and his power, I remember thinking, 'I'm glad I don't have to play against this guy.'"

At Penn State, Harris complemented Mitchell with his ability to run inside or out, giving the Nittany Lions perhaps their best backfield tandem in history.

"Harris was quick enough and had all the moves to be a halfback," said Penn State coach Joe Paterno. "Mitchell was strong and had the straight-ahead power to be a fullback. The outstanding thing about them was their versatility. You could do so much with them because there was nothing they couldn't do."

Before Harris joined Pittsburgh in 1972, championships were a pipe dream in the Steel City.

The Steelers had never won a playoff game. In their first 39 years, they had managed only seven winning seasons and were 14-41-1 in their previous four seasons.

With Harris leading the way as the NFL's offensive rookie of the year, the Steelers did a quick turnaround. He soon became one of the Steelers' most popular players. Fans wearing gear with his number on it were a frequent sight at the stadium.

"The piece that made it all happen was getting a big-time running back like Franco," said former Steelers cornerback Mel Blount.

Each game that the Steelers won gave them more confidence.

"It just built and built and built," running back John "Frenchy" Fuqua said.

You could see the faith growing not only in the players but in the coaches. Still, the season of hope appeared doomed in the playoffs.

With 22 seconds left, the host Steelers trailed the Oakland Raiders 7-6, facing a fourth-and-10 on their 40-yard line with no timeouts left.

Steelers coach Chuck Noll called for a pass play: 66 Circle Option. The play was designed for quarterback Terry Bradshaw to pass to Barry Pearson, a rookie playing in his first NFL game.

Under great pressure, Bradshaw hurriedly threw a long pass to the Raiders' 35. He missed the target, instead passing in Fuqua's direction.

Just as the ball arrived, so did Raiders safety Jack Tatum, known as "The Assassin" for his no-holds-barred hitting. Tatum collided with the Steelers' halfback and knocked Fuqua to the ground. The ball squirted into the air and sailed back end-over-end several yards—into the hands of Harris. He had joined the play to give the desperate Steelers another eligible receiver after first blocking for Bradshaw.

After scooping the ball just before it hit the ground, Harris tore down the sideline to score a touchdown. The stunning play gave the Steelers a 12-7 lead. But first, a question had to be answered: Was the play legal?

It all depended on which player touched the ball first, Fuqua or Tatum, on Bradshaw's heave. If it was Fuqua, the pass would be ruled incomplete because, in those days, offensive players could not consecutively touch a forward pass. If it was Tatum, the TD and Pittsburgh's lead would count.

There was no conclusive evidence in the days long before instant replay reviews.

After a long huddle, officials ruled in favor of the Steelers.

And the "Immaculate Reception" became not only a part of NFL lore, but probably the most famous play in league history.

The game was a turning point for the Steelers, even though they didn't win the 1972 championship. They went on to build a dynasty in the 1970s with their awesome Steel Curtain defense. From 1972–1979, they won four Super Bowls with such stars as Harris, Bradshaw, Jack Ham, Jack Lambert, "Mean Joe" Greene, and Blount.

"The play signifies to me that we weren't the same old Steelers anymore," Harris said in an interview with the *Pittsburgh Tribune Review*. "The same old Steelers would have found a way to lose that playoff game and we found a way to win."

FLUTIE'S WING AND A PRAYER

Doug Flutie had considered himself lucky all his life, so why not now?

Late in the 1984 college football season, the Boston College quarterback had one last chance to pull out a game against the Miami Hurricanes.

There were six seconds left—time for a prayer. Yeah, really, the "Hail Mary" pass.

Everyone in the Orange Bowl stadium in Miami knew it was coming: BC would send all its receivers downfield; Flutie would throw the ball high into the end zone and hope that it ended up with a player wearing the same color uniform. In the Eagles' playbook, it was officially called "55 Flood Tip."

According to Flutie, the play worked "more often than you would think. It's a 50-50." But Flutie could only remember it working one time, against Temple earlier in the season.

Now Flutie hoped he could produce the same result against Miami. Flutie's underdog BC team had put up a strong battle against the defending national champions throughout a rain-splattered day.

The Hurricanes led 45–41 in an explosive back-and-forth game. It was tied 31-31 at the end of three quarters, and the lead changed hands five times in the fourth.

Flutie was matching Miami's Bernie Kosar pass for pass. By the end of the game, Flutie had thrown for 472 yards and Kosar 447.

With BC on the Miami 48-yard line and six ticks on the clock, the Eagles had little choice.

"At this point, I assumed we had lost," said BC coach Jack Bicknell, already thinking what he would say in his emotional postgame speech to his defeated squad.

Flutie was nearing the ending of a glorious career at BC, the only college quarterback in history to pass for 10,000 yards. The 5-foot-9 QB was on his way to the Heisman Trophy in his last season at Boston College.

Strong winds blew and rain pelted the field. And now against Miami, Flutie was ready to throw all caution to the wind, or more precisely, the end zone.

Every eligible receiver for BC streaked downfield. That included Flutie's roommate, Gerard Phelan.

Phelan, one of Flutie's favorite receivers, set himself up directly behind two Miami defenders in the end zone. He had to make sure he was in the end zone, even though he didn't think Flutie could throw the ball that far.

"It wasn't going to be a touchdown if I caught it at the 5-yard line," Phelan said.

Flutie was chased out of the pocket by Hurricanes star defensive lineman Jerome Brown. It was exactly what Flutie wanted.

"The scrambling is important—it gives me the time I need on such a play," Flutie said.

Flutie sidestepped Brown and launched a long pass into the end zone. Somehow, miracle of miracles, the ball finally settled in Phelan's arms after he fought off a crush of players. Flutie didn't even see the completion of the miraculous play.

"I didn't see anything much until the referee raised his arms," Flutie said.

Touchdown!

Boston College 47, Miami 45.

The victory led to a Cotton Bowl berth for the Eagles, which they also won, and a Number 4 ranking in the country.

Flutie went on to a long career in pro football with the NFL, CFL, and USFL. But it was his legendary pass to Phelan that remained one of the greatest moments in American sports history.

Hail Mary?

Better yet, just call it "Hail Flutie."

MAZEROSKI'S MAGIC WAND

Bobby Thomson, Joe Carter, Kirk Gibson—each ballplayer made his mark with a historic post-season home run.

Then there was Bill Mazeroski.

It was the seventh and deciding game of the 1960 World Series. The spotlight was on "Maz" as the Pittsburgh Pirates' all-star second baseman walked to the plate in the bottom of the ninth in a 9-9 game against the New York Yankees.

That the Pirates were still hanging in after six games seemed impossible. The Yankees had dominated the Series in every department but victories.

They had outscored the Pirates 55-27 and outhit them 91-60. Yet the Pirates had split the first six games with the American League champions, who featured a heavy-hitting lineup with the likes of Mickey Mantle, Roger Maris, and Yogi Berra, and a strong pitching staff headed by Whitey Ford.

Mazeroski had always been known more for his glove than his bat.

"To me," said Pirates first baseman Donn Clendenon, "Maz at second is like a businessman having a very efficient secretary. He covers up a lot of my mistakes."

Now his Pirates teammates hoped Maz could get a rally started with his bat. Get on base any way he could: single, walk, hit by a pitch.

On the mound, Ralph Terry peered toward home plate.

Maz took the first pitch from the Yankees' reliever. Ball one.

Maz dug himself into the batter's box.

The windup, the pitch.

Here comes the ball—there it goes, arcing high, higher and even higher, until it lands beyond the covered ivy walls in left.

Home run.

Pirates win, 10-9!

With one swing of Mazeroski's bat, the Pirates were world champions.

The stunned Yankees, who usually ended up on top in World Series play, could only watch in disbelief as Maz circled the bases before a thrilled hometown crowd at Forbes Field. His teammates stormed off the bench to meet him at home plate.

Terry, asked what pitch he had thrown Mazeroski, said, "I don't know what the pitch was. All I know is it was the wrong one."

BOBBY'S WALLOP

We know, we know: some lists ranking the all-time greatest postseason home runs don't put Mazeroski's at the top.

We know all about Coogan's Bluff, the fierce Brooklyn-New York rivalry, and "THE GIANTS WIN THE PENNANT!!!" Yes, Bobby Thomson's "Shot Heard 'Round the World" in the 1951 National League playoffs is generally considered to be the most famous of all.

And before the Miracle at Coogan's Bluff, there was a miraculous comeback by the Giants in the NL race.

On August 11, the Giants trailed the Dodgers by 13 1/2 games and were all but written off by the media and just about everyone else. Said the *New York Times*:

"If the Dodgers even approach their excellent first-half form—and there's no reason why they shouldn't—the battle in the National League from now on will be strictly for second place."

After a while, it was obvious that the Giants were not going to settle for second. They suddenly went on a tear, winning 37 of their last 44 games for an incredible .841 clip.

By the end of the regular season, the Giants had caught up with the Dodgers. The Dodgers needed a great defensive play in the 12th inning and a home run by Jackie Robinson in the 14th to beat Philadelphia and salvage a tie for first for Brooklyn. It set up only the second best-of-three National League playoff series in history.

The Giants beat Brooklyn 3-1 in the first game highlighted by a Thomson home run. The Dodgers came back to tie the series, 10-0, behind the pitching of Clem Labine and an attack that featured four home runs.

The deciding game at the Polo Grounds featured a pitching duel between the Dodgers' Don Newcombe and the Giants' Sal Maglie. The Dodgers held a 4-1 lead going into the ninth with every expectation of winning.

But Newcombe was tiring. Alvin Dark led off the ninth with a single and scooted to third on a single by Don Mueller. After retiring Monte Irvin on a foul pop, Newcombe gave up an RBI double to Whitey Lockman to cut the Dodgers' lead to 4-2.

In came Ralph Branca against Thomson with two men on.

"When I came in to relieve Newcombe, I just kept thinking, 'Get these two guys out and we're in the Series,'" Branca said.

Branca never got the chance to pitch to two batters. Thomson hit Branca's second pitch to him into the left field stands, triggering the famous call of "GIANTS WIN THE PENNANT!" by radio broadcaster Russ Hodges.

Lockman was on second base when Thomson's three-run homer climaxed a three-game playoff and gave the Giants the National League pennant. Years later, Lockman said Thomson hit "the wrong pitch" for the homer that gave the Giants a 5-4 victory over the Dodgers. Lockman said the first offering from Branca was a better pitch to hit, right over the heart of the plate. The second pitch, which Thomson hit into the left field seats at the Polo Grounds, was high.

No matter, in the world of Crazyball, Thomson would forever be a hero in Manhattan and Branca would wear the goat's horns in Brooklyn. In the aftermath of the home run, Thomson and Branca became great friends, usually appearing at memorabilia shows together. They soon realized that they had become a part of something very special.

"Let's face it," Thomson said, "without that moment, we'd both be long forgotten."

A TRULY SICK PERFORMANCE

Picking Michael Jordan's best NBA performance is about as easy as trying to prevent him from having a great night.

Game after game, the Chicago Bulls star just kept topping himself while leading his team to six championships.

Was it the time he scored 63 points against the Boston Celtics in a first-round playoff game in 1986? How about the time he stole the ball from the Utah Jazz in the final minute and hit the winning shot in the 1998 finals, his last title?

Or this: The 1997 playoff game when he crawled out of a sickbed to put the Bulls in position to win their fifth title?

The '97 game with Utah had all the drama you could want.

Coming up was Game 5 of the finals. Jordan woke up that morning with food poisoning or a stomach virus, according to team doctors.

"Standing up was nauseating for him and caused him dizzy spells," Bulls coach Phil Jackson said. "He was completely fatigued and nauseous."

Jordan called his sickness "chill bumps," otherwise known as "goose bumps" or just plain "chills."

In the end, it would be the Jazz who felt ill.

Jordan was not sick enough to stay away from taking the court and playing 44 minutes.

Not only did he score 38 points, he hit the winning 3-point shot with 25 seconds left as the Bulls beat the Jazz in a 90-88 classic.

"In the third quarter, I felt like I couldn't catch my wind and get my energy level up," Jordan said. "I don't know how I got through the fourth quarter. I was just trying to gut myself through it."

Just another walk in the court for the marvelous MJ.

NEW ENGLAND SPORTS CHOWDER

When it comes to special sports moments, players from Boston have had more than their share.

Ted Williams hitting a home run in his last at-bat at Fenway Park. Carlton Fisk winning a World Series game with a 12th-inning homer that he seemed to wave fair as he stood by home plate. Larry Bird dropping 60 on the Atlanta Hawks.

The most lasting image, though, has to be of a hockey player. And for good reason.

When a photographer captured Boston's Bobby Orr scoring his Stanley Cup-winning goal against the St. Louis Blues in 1970, it soon became hard to forget. Impossible, in fact.

The picture in black and white shows Orr frozen in flight in front of the net, his stick held high, after beating goaltender Glenn Hall. The goal in overtime was voted the greatest moment in NHL history.

"Honest, I don't know how it went in," said Orr, an offensive-minded defenseman who made scoring goals second nature.

Orr brought a different perspective to defensemen when he entered the NHL in 1966. They were normally expected to "stay at home" and protect their own end and their goalie first. Orr, on the other hand, added more athleticism and brought sizzling speed and scoring ability to the position. His end-to-end rushes were breathtaking.

He was the most dynamic player of his time, an attack-first defenseman, opening the door for other great rushing defensemen such as Paul Coffey and Ray Bourque, another Boston superstar who has also had his special moments.

Many think Orr might have been the greatest hockey player of all.

"I loved to carry the puck, I always played like that since I was a kid," said Orr, who came rushing out of Parry Sound, Ontario, to change the game of hockey. There had been other rushing defensemen before Orr, but none that produced the startling numbers Orr did.

Before Orr, there had never been a defenseman who led the league in scoring—Orr did it twice. (His 120 points in the 1969-70 season broke the record for a defenseman by a ridiculous 56 points.)

Before Orr, there had never been a player in the NHL who scored over 100 points—Orr did it six times.

He practically owned the Norris Trophy, winning it eight straight years as the NHL's top defenseman.

In a 12-year career, mostly with the Bruins, Orr scored 270 goals and assisted on 645 for 915 points in just 657 games.

Orr's NHL career could not be defined by numbers. When he was on the ice, he was usually the center of attention. His ability to simply take over a game and will his team to victory was wondrous to behold.

One game typified his impact: Orr scored one goal, set up another, and almost single-handedly killed the other team's power play by controlling the puck all by himself.

Quipped Orr's teammate Derek Sanderson: "Bobby controlled the puck for 40 minutes and let the other 35 players in the game use it for the other 20."

In the 1970 Stanley Cup Finals, Orr was in attack mode again. His Bruins were going for a sweep of the St. Louis Blues and their first Cup since 1941.

After Boston blowouts in the first three games, Game 4 was more competitive; the teams tied 3-3 after regulation. Early in OT, the 22-year-old Orr set things in motion by beating the Blues' Larry Keenan to a loose puck. He passed to Sanderson in the corner, then dashed toward the crease.

Sanderson slid the puck back to Orr as the defenseman charged across the crease. The old give-and-go.

"As I skated across [Hall] had to move across the crease and had to open his pads a little," Orr said.

Orr somehow slipped the puck between Hall's legs, then went into flight when tripped by the Blues' Noel Picard.

Snap.

The image of Orr in flight was captured by photographer Ray Lussier of the *Boston Record American.*

The Bruins had their Stanley Cup, with a *Mona Lisa*–caliber picture to prove it.

GRANTING A WISH

Grant Hill held the fate of the Duke Blue Devils in his hands. Literally.

"Can you make the pass?" Duke coach Mike Krzyzewski asked Hill.

"Yeah, coach, I can do it."

Coach K turned to Christian Laettner.

"Can you catch it?"

Laettner nodded.

There were 2.1 seconds left in overtime and the Blue Devils trailed the Kentucky Wildcats by one point. Duke had time for one last desperation play.

The stakes were high in this 1992 NCAA Eastern Regional final in Philadelphia: win and go to the Final Four, lose and go home.

It would practically take a miracle for Duke to win. Duke broadcaster Bob Harris watched the Blue Devils take their positions on the court.

"The first thing that hit my mind was 'Wake Forest. We're going to do the same thing.'"

Earlier in the season the Blue Devils tried a similar play against Wake Forest, a nearly full-court pass by Hill for the deciding basket. It didn't work.

Now another try for Hill. The Duke forward stood at one end line, waiting to make an inbounds pass to Laettner at the other end. Laettner had set himself up some 75 feet away, waiting to receive Hill's baseball-like pass, waiting to be a hero.

Remarkably, no one was guarding Hill, and Kentucky's defenders were behind Laettner.

The pass better be perfect this time, Hill thought.

That the outcome was being decided in the final seconds of overtime was appropriate. So far it had been one of the greatest games ever in the NCAA playoffs. Kentucky had just moved in front 103-102 on a strange-looking shot by Sean Woods that found the net. It was the fourth lead change in less than a minute.

Laettner had not missed a shot all day, going 9 for 9 from the field and 10 for 10 from the foul line. *This is no time to break the streak*, he thought. As Laettner took up his position, he was "a little nervous about it."

"I remember saying to myself, 'Just get a good shot up.' We had done that play in practice a few times during the year. I don't know if I ever made it in practice."

Hill's pass went up. As an excited Harris described it on the broadcast:

"The l-on-g pass. Laettner goes up. Catches . . . comes down, turns, dribbles, shoots!"

The ball dropped through the basket.

"SCORES!"

Final: Duke 104, Kentucky 103.

The "Greatest Game Ever" was on everybody's lips. It would be hard to top, for sure.

MILLER TIME

Spike Lee was gloating, and could you blame him?

It was the opener of the NBA's Eastern Conference semi-final series in 1995 and his New York Knicks were leading the Indiana Pacers by six points with just 18.7 seconds left. Lee, the moviemaker and passionate Knicks fan, had a personal and very public feud with the Pacers' Reggie Miller.

There was a history of hard feelings between these teams, as well. In the 1994 playoffs, Miller scored 25 points in the fourth quarter to beat the Knicks, then flashed the "choke" sign to Lee.

Only to see the Knicks win that series.

Then came the 1995 playoffs, the most remarkable performance of all by Indiana's sharpshooting guard.

It was in the final minute of the game. Madison Square Garden was rocking, the crowd uplifted by a foul call on Rick

Smits that had sent the Pacers center to the bench. Smits had done everything he could to beat the Knicks, scoring 34 points and holding New York's all-star center, Patrick Ewing, to 11.

"We were pretty down," Smits said.

But Miller was thinking in a different direction.

"When you're down by six with fifteen, twenty seconds left, it doesn't look good," Miller said. "But you can never give up."

Miller figured if the Pacers could get a quick 3-pointer, they still might have a chance. So guess what: Miller received the inbounds pass, turned, and connected for a 3-pointer. The Knicks' lead was now three points.

Knicks forward Anthony Mason attempted to throw the ball inbounds, but made an awful errant pass. Miller was there to scoop up the basketball.

"I didn't know he was going to throw it right in my hands," Miller said.

The Indiana star had the presence of mind to step back beyond the 3-point line. He tied the game with another shot.

Remarkably, Miller had made two 3-pointers in a span of 3.1 seconds.

The game was now tied 105-105, the crowd stunned. The fans quieted as the Knicks' John Starks missed two foul shots and Ewing missed a following layup.

Miller was fouled. He stepped to the line and calmly hit two free throws to give the hated Pacers a 107-105 victory.

A performance for the ages for Miller: an incredible eight points in just nine seconds.

Now it was Miller's turn to gloat and cry out, "Choke artists! Choke artists!"

"I love playing here in the Garden," he said. "The atmosphere, the media, the fans—I love how they dog us out. It's a good rivalry."

A SOLID GOLD PERFORMANCE

Downhill skier Franz Klammer retired from elite competition in 1985 with a record 25 career World Cup victories. He is most remembered for his spectacular run that won him a gold medal at the 1976 Innsbruck Olympics, a performance on which Klammer was on the edge, even sometimes over it, as he sped down the mountainside.

It wasn't pretty. Indeed, it was reckless: Klammer sailed through the air with his arms and legs flailing, looking like anything but a gold medal winner. But when he reached the bottom of the hill, in front of his Austrian countrymen yelling themselves hoarse in support—an estimated crowd of 60,000—Klammer won by .33 of a second.

The race became a staple of ABC's Winter Olympics highlights packages through the years. A U.S. customs agent once told Klammer, "I remember you. You're the man who almost killed himself that day."

ROARING TIGER

It takes a lot to impress Jack Nicklaus, golf's all-time leader with 18 majors.

Tiger Woods did just that at the Nicklaus-hosted Memorial tournament in 2012.

"I've seen a lot of shots in golf," Nicklaus said. "I don't think I've seen a better one."

Nicklaus referred to a shot that Tiger made on a late charge that added another US PGA Tour victory to his résumé. His 73rd win on the tour tied Tiger with Nicklaus, second on the all-time list behind Sam Snead's 82.

The highlight of Tiger's charge:

With a tough lie above the hole and a slick downhill green before a water hazard, Tiger holed a chip shot out of a thick rough on Muirfield Village's 16th.

Tiger at his best.

"That was the most unbelievable gutsy shot I've ever seen," Nicklaus said. "If he is short, the tournament is over. If he's long the tournament is over, and he put it in the hole."

OLYMPIC ACHIEVEMENT

On the night before the 1968 Mexico Olympic Games, long jumper Bob Beamon was nervous. He couldn't sleep, so he went into town and hit some bars.

He was relaxed, very relaxed, when it came time to compete.

"My mind was blank," he said. "After so much jumping, jumping becomes automatic."

Jumping out of the stadium is another matter, however.

Not even Beamon expected what happened next. All he did was add nearly two feet to the 27 foot, 4 3/4 inches record in one leap. He soared 29, 2 1/2, entirely skipping the 28-foot barrier on his way.

How unusual was it? Long jump records usually advanced by the odd inch or two. Pretty much still do.

It took 23 years before his record was broken.

"I was as surprised as anyone at the distance," Beamon said.

6

CHUCKLEBALL

Make them laugh, make them cry. And it doesn't have to make any sense, either.

If you're wondering what exactly makes for a successful sports movie—we're not talking artistic fulfillment here—try belly laughs, absurd characters and plots, and big stars.

We don't mean Kevin Costner and Gene Hackman, either. More like the goofballs who appeal to the baser instincts in moviegoers. In all of us, really.

You know the names, and we don't even have to repeat them here. Simply listing the titles of the big moneymakers in sports films should suffice:

The Waterboy
The Longest Yard
Talladega Nights: The Ballad of Ricky Bobby
Blades of Glory
Dodgeball: A True Underdog Story
Nacho Libre

Fans filled the theaters for those yuckfests, many of which had premises so absurd that, well, they required Adam Sandler, Will Ferrell, Ben Stiller, or Jack Black to have top billing.

As Chazz Michael Michaels (Ferrell, of course) says in the figure skating comedy *Blades of Glory*—wait, figure skating comedy? Well, yeah, if you can pull off men's pairs the way Ferrell and Jon Heder do:

"They laughed at Louis Armstrong when he said he was going to the moon, and now he's laughing at them from up there."

Make any sense? Uh, no.

Make us laugh? You bet!

If you can stop laughing from their outlandish antics long enough, though, try recognizing some of the classic comedies based on sports:

Caddyshack and *Major League*.

Cool Runnings and *The Bad News Bears*.

Even *Kingpin* and *Horse Feathers*.

And, of course, *Slap Shot*.

Herewith, some of the oddball occurrences, great scenes, and dialogue from the classic (and crappy) sports films that made us convulse with laughter or shield our eyes and cover our ears, wondering, "Did they really just do that?"

SLAP SHOT

If it's not the greatest hockey movie, it certainly is the wackiest, even if the classy superstar Paul Newman led the cast and accomplished filmmaker George Roy Hill (*The Sting*, *Butch Cassidy and the Sundance Kid*) directed it.

And the true whack jobs were the Hanson brothers.

Played by real-life hockey players Steve and Jeff Carlson and Dave Hanson—they have their own website (www.hansonbrothers.net)—their time in hockey's minor leagues actually was the catalyst for the film, written by Nancy Dowd, the sister of a teammate. Not only are the Charlestown Chiefs and their veteran player-coach Reggie Dunlop, played by Newman, based on a real team (the Johnstown, Pennsylvania, Jets), but there's plenty of authenticity in the personas of the goon-it-up screen siblings.

Dave Hanson wound up as one of the battling brothers because a real Carlson, Jack, had been called up to the NHL and was unavailable for filming. Perhaps Jack lost his shot at celluloid immortality, but he did play 12 pro seasons.

Of course, the guys in *Slap Shot* have played to worldwide audiences since the film was released in 1977, bringing the kind of fame they surely wouldn't have drawn otherwise. There were no Stanley Cups in the futures of Dave Hanson or the Carlsons, although they did make it to the Hockey Hall of Fame as part of an exhibit about the movie.

The Hansons claim they ate beef jerky and drank root beer as their pregame meals; who's to doubt that? And their ritual before the game included, well, something out of the pages of the "What Can We Get Away With?" manual.

"We taped our hands like boxers until the leagues banned it. After that, we scuffed up the knuckles of golf gloves, soaked them in water, and dried them on the radiator until they were nice and crispy. We made sure that we got in a fight on our first shift because they softened up after we started sweating."

They're kidding. Maybe.

Classic Scene: As all hell breaks loose on the ice, Ned Braden, played by Michael Ontkean, instead decides to do a striptease. Sportscaster Jim Carr (Andrew Duncan) can't believe what he is seeing: "He's not fighting! No, he's . . . Ned Braden is starting to take off articles of his uniform!"

Classic line: During the national anthem, the referee warns Steve Hanson he will have none of the bloodletting the Chiefs have become infamous for. Steve replies straight-faced and with total disrespect.

Referee: "I got my eye on the three of you guys. I run a clean game here"

Steve: "I'm listenin' to the f-----g song"

MAJOR LEAGUE

There are more authentic and acclaimed baseball movies. None comes close to the raucous hilarity of the Cleveland Indians—who can be pretty funny, in a sad way, with their actual exploits in the American League.

A perfectly cast group ranging from the wily veteran catcher trying to hang on (Tom Berenger as Jake Taylor) to the hotshot pitcher with the howitzer arm and pea brain (Charlie Sheen as Ricky "Wild Thing" Vaughn), *Major League* is Crazyball personified. In the dugout, on the field, in the broadcast booth, and in the owners' box.

Written by lifelong Indians fan David S. Ward, whose screenplay for *The Sting* won an Oscar, it was Ward's way of getting the Indians out of the basement.

"I grew up in Cleveland," Ward told *Sports Illustrated*. "I remember the 1954 World Series and how upset my father was that the Indians, after such a spectacular season (111-43), were swept by the Giants. That's when I realized how important a baseball game could be.

"After that, things went into a decline in Cleveland. Just grim, awful, hopeless years. I thought, 'The only way the Indians will ever win anything in my lifetime is if I make a movie where they do.' And obviously it has to be a comedy because nobody would believe it as a drama."

Among the brilliantly conceived characters were Vaughn, who spent the previous year in the California Penal League; Cuban slugger Pedro Cerrano (Dennis Haysbert), a voodoo worshipper befuddled by the breaking stuff; base-stealing artist Willie Mays Hayes (Wesley Snipes), whose ability to show off matched his ego as well as his raw speed; over-the-hill spitballer Eddie Harris (Chelcie Ross); manager Lou Brown (James Gammon), who never met a hunch he wouldn't try; team owner Rachel Phelps (Margaret Whitton), who hatches the plan to create the worst team in sports history so she can move it out of Cleveland; and play-by-play man Harry Doyle.

Bob Uecker perfectly fit the Doyle part. Equal parts former player, current announcer, and full-time humorist, Uecker didn't need a script to describe the action—or lack of it.

"They told me to do whatever you want," Doyle, uh, Uecker said. "You don't have to follow the script. They just said, 'The Indians are getting their asses kicked every day; have fun with it.' So I did. My stuff was funny."

As was just about everything about *Major League*.

Classic Scene: Brown places a cardboard pin-up of the owner in the locker room and proclaims with a smirk: "Every time we win, we peel a section." The Indians win and win and win.

Soon, they are doing an American Express commercial that Hayes completes by sliding across home plate, looking into the camera, and saying: "Don't steal home without it."

Classic Line: As Vaughn's struggles continue, one pitch gets sent into orbit. Taylor tries to console him:

> Taylor: "That ball wouldn't have been out of a lot of parks."
>
> Vaughn: "Name one."
>
> Taylor: "Yellowstone?"

CADDYSHACK

That Bill Murray became a golfing icon has nothing—and everything—to do with his creation of the Dalai Lama's favorite loopy looper, Carl Spackler.

But Murray's stoner assistant groundskeeper is just one of the, oh, 18 or so great characters in Harold Ramis's unforgettably funny 1980 romp through Bushwood Country Club. One for every hole.

Such as Rodney Dangerfield's Al Czervik, whose golf bag comes equipped with a draught beer tap, TV, radio, and hydraulic club lifter.

Or Chevy Chase's Ty Webb, the not-as-suave-as-he-thinks golf pro with the nerves of jelly who at one point we see supposedly lining up a putt when he's actually taking a leak on the course.

From Ted Knight's obnoxious, cheating Judge Smails to his niece, Lacey Underalls—the name says it all for Cindy Morgan's teasing fox—to Henry Wilcoxon's not-particularly-pious Bishop, every portrayal is as pinpoint as a Tiger Woods wedge.

Caddyshack was the creation of first-time director Ramis and several other writers he worked with on *Animal House*. One of the cowriters, Bryan Doyle Murray (caddymaster Lou Loomis), pitched a film in the *Animal House* genre about an upscale golf club and, basically, how to destroy it.

"My brother, Bill, and I worked on a golf course and had been caddies," Bryan Doyle Murray said. "It was a ripe target for that kind of project."

Because *Saturday Night Live* had become must-watch television for the younger generation of that time, hiring Chase and Bill Murray was a brilliant stroke, just as casting John Belushi as Blutarsky was in *Animal House*.

Letting Murray loose to ad-lib—Ramis said Murray had no scripted lines—and letting Dangerfield spread his hilariously harmless insults everywhere also were critical to the film.

But producer Jon Peters and Ramis knew they were taking some chances. For one, Dangerfield was a successful stand-up comic known to America for short stints on TV variety shows. Could he carry a character through an entire movie?

Would Knight's performance come off as a ripoff of his Ted Baxter persona on *The Mary Tyler Moore Show*?

Would the part played by Morgan, who was a radio disc jockey before auditioning for the role, hold up?

And what about the Chase–Bill Murray dynamic? Murray actually replaced Chase on *SNL*, and there was little previous camaraderie between them. Indeed, there were some hard feelings.

The filmmakers got around that by not having them shoot scenes together. Except, of course, the bit where Chase hits a ball into Murray's, uh, abode, and asks if he can "play through." The ball landed on Murray's "special turf," a grass that could be either planted or smoked.

That byplay between the two comics was totally unscripted, and both admitted they barely avoided bursting out in laughter during it.

Then again, that was common for this movie. Shot in Florida in 11 weeks at a cost of $6 million, *Caddyshack* has become, well, priceless among comedies—and not just sports comedies.

As Chase told *Sports Illustrated*:

"I don't know why it's stuck around so long. It's a funny movie, it had funny stars, it had Harold and great writing. All of that should be enough to make a movie memorable to a certain crowd. But I don't think it's about golf—it's about class: snobs versus slobs.

"Is it the funniest sports movie ever? Maybe. I can't imagine there was a Babe Ruth movie that was funnier."

Classic Scene: Bishop Pickerling opts to "squeeze in nine holes before this rain starts." He appoints Spackler to carry his bag, and off they go.

The bishop starts knocking shots next to and into the hole as lightning bolts fill the sky and thunder crackles all around. Other golfers flee the course, but Pickerling believes he can break the club record. So on he and Spackler traipse, after Carl insists "the heavy stuff won't come down for a while." By heavy stuff, he must have meant a typhoon.

The bishop says "The Good Lord would never disrupt the best game of my life," and he is right—until the last hole.

Pickerling's putt scoots through the deluge and past the cup. He points his putter to the sky, curses the gods, and immediately is struck down by lightning.

Spackler drops the flag and the golf bag and skulks away, with the bishop's body supine on the putting surface.

Classic Line: Head groundskeeper Sandy McFiddish (Thomas Carlin) gives Spackler his marching orders.

Sandy: "Carl, I want you to kill all the gophers on the golf course."

Carl: "Correct me if I am wrong, Sandy, but if I kill all the golfers, they'll lock me up and throw away the key."

Sandy: "Not golfers, you great fool. Gophers. The little brown, furry rodents."

Carl: "We can do that. We don't even need a reason."

HORSE FEATHERS

Academia meets the Marx Brothers. And a football game breaks out.

Well, something that resembles a football game, with the additions of cigars, rubber bands, banana peels, hidden ball tricks, and typical Marxian mayhem.

Groucho's Professor Quincy Wagstaff is hired to get Huxley College headed back in the right direction. His nihilistic plan: "I'm Against It."

He sings about the faculty:

"I don't know what they have to say, it makes no difference anyway.

"Whatever it is, I'm against it."

That's the starting point for a Marx Brothers classic which, like *A Day at the Races*, has a sports theme.

The brothers would do anything for a laugh, lampooning long before there was a *National Lampoon* such subjects as politics, the military, the arts, and, yes, sports. And while the gridiron scene in *Horse Feathers* is as farcical—and hilarious—as moviemaking can get, it also delivers a message about the absurd emphasis placed on college football.

And this was in 1932!

Classic Scene: What else but the most ridiculous gridiron farce on celluloid?

Groucho determines that the best way for Huxley to beat archrival Darwin is to fix the game. He dispatches henchmen Chico and Harpo to kidnap the two stars of the Darwin team, a plan doomed from the beginning—but destined to work just fine, as in all Marx Brothers films as they bumble their way to victory.

Groucho gives a pregame pep talk. Not to his own team, which he claims wouldn't listen to him, but to the Darwin players.

Because the kidnapping scheme failed, Darwin is able to take a 12-0 lead. But Huxley has some secret weapons:

Harpo tying a long rubber band around the ball, then throwing it to Chico, who sends it right back to his brother even as the Darwin players go to tackle Chico. Harpo runs down the sideline for a touchdown.

The four brothers line up and each kicks the other's backside until Zeppo puts the extra point through the uprights. Darwin 12, Huxley 7.

Things really go bananas the next time Huxley has the ball. As Zeppo runs down the left sideline, Harpo tosses banana peels in the way of pursuing opponents. Of course, he also throws some at Zeppo's feet and the youngest Marx brother goes down short of the goal line.

Chico barks out the next signals: "Hi-Diddle-Diddle, the cat and the fiddle, this time I think we go through the middle."

Typically, Harpo runs left instead and is in the clear—until a dog comes sprinting the other way on the field. Harpo's canine-catcher instincts take hold and he gives chase, with the three other Marxes chasing him.

Somehow, there's a chariot in the end zone and the brothers all climb in, forget the pooch, and ride to the Darwin end zone for the winning TD.

For emphasis, they place down football after football as the scoreboard tote rises.

Classic Line: Professor Wagstaff addresses the faculty about the dilemma faced by Huxley.

Wagstaff: "This college is a failure. The trouble is, we're neglecting football for education."

Faculty members: "Exactly, the professor is right."

Wagstaff: "Oh, I'm right, am I? Well, I'm not right. I'm wrong. I just said that to test you. Now I know where I'm at. I'm dealing with a couple of snakes. What I meant to say was that there's too much football and not enough education."

Faculty members: "That's what I think."

Wagstaff: "Oh, you do, do you? Well, you're wrong again. If there was a snake, you'd apologize. Where would this college be without football? Have we got a stadium?"

Faculty members: "Yes."

Wagstaff: "Have we got a college?"

Faculty members: "Yes."

Wagstaff: "Well, we can't support both. Tomorrow we start tearing down the college."

Faculty members: "But Professor, where will the students sleep?"

Wagstaff: "Where they always sleep: in the classroom."

TALLADEGA NIGHTS: THE BALLAD OF RICKY BOBBY

We learned long ago that Will Ferrell will skewer any subject, with sports being among his favorite topics to destroy. Nothing is sacred for the man who founded the website FunnyorDie.com, won the 2011 Mark Twain Prize for American Humor, and has as loyal a following as, well, Dale Earnhardt Jr.

So when Ferrell and partner in comedic crime John C. Reilly decided to annihilate NASCAR, well, it might not be Crazyball, but it's wild stuff with a good ol' boy flavor.

The speed demons also hilariously drive deep into the corners of gay-bashing (with ultimate acceptance of all lifestyles), home-wrecking, loyalty, patriotism, and, because it's NASCAR, sponsorships. Just think how many times we saw Wonder Bread (Ricky Bobby), Old Spice (Cal Naughton Jr., played by O'Reilly), and Perrier (Jean Girard, portrayed flamboyantly by Sacha Baron Cohen) on screen. Those products got more exposure during the film than they could ever hope for in a real race. And they didn't pay a penny to get it.

If only auto racing fans were the ones spending their pennies and dollars to see *Talladega Nights*, it would have been a hit. Had only Ferrell fans gone, it would have been a success. But the combination, along with the absurd action, drove Ricky Bobby and company to the top of box office charts in the summer of 2006.

"When we pitched the idea, the studios were lining up" Ferrell said.

Presumably not in front of his No. 26 car.

Ferrell's dimwitted character, whose father abandoned him as a child with the words "If you ain't first, you're last," uses that advice to climb his way to the top of stock car racing. Along the way, he befriends Naughton, who so worships Bobby that he gladly accepts "shaking and baking" to second place to his pal's Number One—*every time*!

Bobby's world is shattered first by the appearance of the "French Flamer," Girard, a Formula 1 driver who takes NASCAR by storm. Then a crash takes away Bobby's nerves and taste for speed.

"We had fun with the sport, but we didn't poke fun at the sport," Ferrell said. "It's a mixture. We had a lot of people in early screenings, a lot of our kind of colleagues in Hollywood . . . who said, 'Wow, you guys make the sport look great, like I want to go see a race now.' It's a comedy movie, so you want to go laugh at stuff that's involved with NASCAR and that sort of thing."

Classic Scene: Ricky Bobby finally climbs back into his car after his horrific crash, from which he was convinced he was paralyzed even though doctors told him otherwise. During that first practice at Rockingham Speedway, he immediately revs the car up to an incredible . . . 26 mph. Ricky thinks he is motoring along at supersonic speeds.

When the other guys fly past him, he freaks out.

"Am I on fire?" he asks as he climbs from the car in the pits.

"You're not on fire," everyone insists.

Doesn't matter. He strips down to his underwear—his racing helmet still on, of course—runs onto the track and does windmills as his crew members chase him down.

Classic Line: Bobby and Naughton are confronted at the racetrack by Girard, who first is sympathetic to Bobby's injuries. Then the conversation turns ugly.

Naughton: "I got a message for all of 'em—Shake and Bake."

Bobby: "What does that do? Does that blow your mind? That just happened!"

Girard: "What is that, a catchphrase? Or some kind of epilepsy?"

HAPPY GILMORE

Adam Sandler once was voted one of the top 20 celebrity athletes. His love for basketball is well known: Sandler often shows up at NBA games and has done promotions for the league.

He's been a football player in prison (*The Longest Yard*) and in college (*The Waterboy*). Hoops provided the impetus for a reunion of old *Saturday Night Live* buddies in *Grown Ups*.

But Sandler was at his most outlandish portraying the failed hockey player Happy Gilmore, who discovers he can translate some of his ice skills to the golf course—and save his grandmother's house by doing so.

Happy has had a less-than-happy life so far. His father was so obsessed with hockey that Happy's mother left him and their son and moved—to Egypt, no less. Then his dad takes a puck to the head and is killed.

He's brought up by his beloved grandmother, but lacks discipline. How so? Well, when he is cut at hockey tryouts, he gets into a fight with the coach. When the IRS shows up to take Grandma's house, Happy throws the agent out—no, through—the front door.

As his grandmother is dispossessed and moving men prepare to take her to a nursing home, Happy is enraged to find the workers hitting golf balls. They refuse to get back to work unless Happy can hit the ball farther than they do.

So using his slapshot form, Happy rockets the ball, oh, 400 yards. Naturally, he breaks a window down the street. Then he conks people on the head with longer drives.

Discovering his unknown talent and desperately needing money, he heads to the driving range, where he eventually teams with former pro Chubbs Peterson (Carl Weathers), who has a fake hand; the real one was bitten off by an alligator.

Off Happy heads to the pro tour, seeking enough money to buy back Granny's home.

Will he succeed? After a tortuous journey, of course. He'll even find love.

Classic Scene: Come On Down!!!

Happy is teamed with ever-smiling *The Price Is Right* host Bob Barker in a pro-am. Happy is playing like a clueless bidder from the game show, though.

And he is being heckled constantly by a fan, prompting Happy to complain to Barker that the fan "is driving me crazy." Barker responds that Happy "not getting the ball in the hole" is driving him crazy.

Barker tells Happy he should be working at the snack bar, not impersonating a professional golfer. He then insists that Happy couldn't have been as bad at hockey as he is at golf.

Happy drops the gloves, uh, golf club, says, "All right, let's go," and decks Barker with a right cross.

Oliver (Patsy) Tebeau played for the Cleveland Spiders, but escaped their worst season in 1899 when Frank Robison sent him (along with many of the Spiders' best players) to the St. Louis Perfectos. Library of Congress, Goodwin & Company, LC-DIG-bbc-0176f

Ted Williams finished the 1941 season by setting a new standard at .406. Photo courtesy of The Baseball Collection

“Shoeless” Joe Jackson, who was banned from the game for life after being accused, with several teammates, of throwing the 1919 World Series. Library of Congress, George Grantham Bain Collection, LC-DIG-ggbain-25393

Michael Jordan, when sick with either a stomach virus or food poisoning, went on to play for 44 minutes and scored 38 points (plus the winning three-point shot) to put the Bulls in position to win their fifth title. Photo courtesy of Jason H. Smith

George Stallings, the superstitious manager of the 1914 Miracle Braves. Library of Congress, George Grantham Bain Collection, LC-DIG-ggbain-17329

Babe Ruth to the Yankees—one of the worst "trades" in baseball history. Library of Congress, Underwood & Underwood, LC-USZ62-71763

Jason Giambi. Who would guess he sported a gold lamé thong when he was in a slump? Photo courtesy of Keith Allison

Wilt "the Stilt" Chamberlain, who played for the theatrical Harlem Globetrotters. Library of Congress, *New York World-Telegram* and the *Sun Newspaper* Photograph Collection, LC-USZ62-115428

The San Diego Chicken. Photo courtesy of J. Chris Vaughan

Yogi Berra (left), a man as notable for his baseball career as for his famous double-talk. Courtesy of the Trustees of the Boston Public Library/Leslie Jones Collection

Winston Churchill, who had a particular disdain for the sport of golf. Library of Congress, LC-USW33-019093-C

The Reverend Billy Graham, who once said: "The only time my prayers are never answered is on the golf course." Library of Congress, Warren K. Leffler, U.S. News & World Report Magazine Photograph Collection, LC-DIG-ppmsc-03261

"You want a piece of me?" Happy shouts at Barker, who gets up, responds "I don't want a piece of you; I want the whole thing," and proceeds to pummel Happy as if he were beating up a rag doll.

They wind up tumbling down a hill as they wrestle, and Happy head-butts Barker, seemingly knocking him unconscious.

"The Price Is Wrong, bitch," Happy declares.

But Barker is hardly done, doing a Mike Tyson on Gilmore and then finishing it off with a kick to the jaw that would make any martial arts champion proud.

Guess the price was right for Barker, after all.

Classic Line: Chubbs tells Happy why he didn't make it as a pro.

Chubbs: "Back in 1965, *Sports Illustrated* said I was going to be the next Arnold Palmer."

Happy: "Yeah? What happened?"

Chubbs: "They wouldn't let me play on the pro tour anymore."

Happy: "Ah, I'm sorry. Because you're black?"

Chubbs: "Hell no! Damned alligator bit my hand off."

Happy: "Oh my God!!!!"

Chubbs: "Yeah. Tournament down in Florida. I hooked my ball in the rough down by the lake. Damned alligator just popped up, cut me down in my prime. He got me, but I tore one of that bastard's eyes out though. Look at that." [He shows Happy a glass jar with an eyeball in it.]

Happy: "You're pretty sick, Chubbs."

COOL RUNNINGS

Loosely based on a true story—yeah, mon, Jamaica did have a national bobsled team compete in the Olympics—*Cool Runnings* is as much about culture shock of a frigid nature as it is about sports.

It's also, by far, the funniest taste of tobogganing you will get anywhere.

And the plot actually makes sense. Or it does if anyone truly believes the Caribbean is the place to find Winter Olympics athletes.

John Candy plays Irv Blitzer, who cheated at the Olympics and lost his gold medal because he added illegal weight to the sled. Derice Bannock (played by Leon—one name only; perhaps Leon believed he was a Brazilian soccer player) also had Olympic misfortune, but not of his own doing. He was tripped by another runner, Junior Bevil (Rawle D. Lewis) while trying to qualify in the 100-yard dash.

Bannock, the son of a gold medalist, hooks up with Blitzer, now a bookie, in a scheme to get each of them to the 1988 Calgary Games. As the Jamaican bobsled squad.

One of Bannock's friends is Sanka Coffie (no cream, just sugar, please), played by Doug E. Doug. Coffie is a champion pushcart racer, the fastest on the island.

Bannock eventually recruits Coffie to the team, although all Coffie wants to do, naturally, is drive. Another volunteer is the very bald Yul Brenner (Malik Yoba), another sprinter who failed to qualify for the Olympics.

And the fourth member? Bevil, because nobody else shows up for tryouts, and you can't have a four-man team without, ahem, four men.

Coffie eventually becomes the brakeman so Bannock can drive, and off they go on their pursuit of Olympic glory.

Their comical sidesteps include crashing into a police car during training. Along with several fundraisers, Bevil sells his car to finally get enough money for the trip to Calgary.

But the Jamaicans have no sled; Blitzer winds up buying an old used one from the American team. They have nowhere to practice and wind up on a hockey rink.

And when they show up at the bobsled track, things go so badly that, at one point, all four of them are seen running down the track chasing the sled.

Three of the guys eventually get into a bar fight with a German team, and Bevil is ordered by his father to come back home. But he stays, Blitzer gets them back on track, and they actually qualify to compete.

Even as they celebrate, though, they are disqualified: The Jamaicans never competed in an international race before the Olympics. But Blitzer persuades the judges to reverse their ruling, the Jamaican bobsledders march in the opening ceremony, then compete in the Games, to strong support from the fans.

The sled is in no racing condition, and they crash. Determined not to end their Olympics this way, the four Jamaicans pick up the sled on their shoulders and walk to the finish line.

Classic Scene: To the sounds of steel drums and reggae, the team takes off from Jamaica. The music changes to twangy country as the plane lands on the snowy runway in Calgary.

They arrive in the terminal and, led by Irv, step out into the blustery breeze that doesn't in any way resemble the Jamaican climate.

Not exactly step out, actually. All four of the Jamaicans freeze at the exit door. Sanka runs back inside, opens his knapsack, and proceeds to put on every piece of clothing in it. And a blanket, to boot.

Then they pile into a bus as Irv asks incredulously: "What's the matter, you guys cold?"

The airport sign shows minus-25 degrees (Centigrade or Fahrenheit, that is C-O-L-D!).

Classic Line: Derice explains to Sanka the, uh, joys of bobsledding.

Derice: "The key elements to a successful sled team are a steady driver and three strong runners to push off down the ice."

Sanka: "ICE? ICE!"

Derice: "Well, it's kind of a winter sport, you know."

Sanka: "You mean winter, as in ice?"

Derice: "Possibly."

Sanka: "You mean winter, as in igloos and Eskimos and penguins and ICE?"

Derice: "Maybe."

Sanka: "See ya."

THE BAD NEWS BEARS

Any film starring Walter Matthau immediately promises chuckles, guffaws, and belly laughs. Casting the veteran comedy actor as drunken washout former minor leaguer Morris Buttermaker and having him manage a group of wise-ass misfit baseball players—that's genius.

Little League has become far too serious of a game or business, and even back in 1976 it was headed in that direction. Too much parent interference, too many coaches/managers acting out their major league fantasies—you know the drill.

So when director Michael Ritchie opted to throw a few beanballs at the youth level, it was funny and well-deserved. It also spawned three sequels and a TV series, none of which came close to the original.

Buttermaker initally has about as much interest in coaching these kids as Matthau would have had in portraying Hamlet. And this is a team made up of the least athletic Little Leaguers imaginable. Giving true meaning to Little Leaguer, shortstop Tanner Boyle (Chris Barnes) has a complex about his height—and a filthy mouth. The catcher Engelberg (Gary Lee Cavagnaro) has enough of his own padding to not need the usual protective equipment. One of the pitchers is so nearsighted he can't see home plate from the mound.

Though he is getting paid by one of the parents, Buttermaker doesn't do much to encourage this motley crew, and they don't even get one out when losing 26-0 in their first game. Indeed, Buttermaker forfeits when the score reaches 26.

At that point, Buttermaker could just walk away. What kind of Hollywood ending would that be? Instead, he decides to fight back against the Little League establishment, particularly haughty, hateful manager Roy Turner of the Yankees.

As he reasons, "This quitting thing, it's a hard habit to break once you start."

So Buttermaker turns recruiter, bringing in a quick-with-a-quip 12-year-old pitcher named Amanda (yes, a girl, played delightfully by Tatum O'Neal). Buttermaker and Amanda had a history. When she was younger, he had trained her to pitch, and she was somebody he actually cared about. Amanda, the daughter of one of Buttermaker's former girlfriends, insists she be compensated with ballet lessons and imported jeans, among other demands.

Then he persuades Kelly Leak (Jackie Earle Haley, who actually looks like he knows his way around a diamond) to play. That Leak rides a motorcycle, smokes, and has a job as a loan shark, all while barely a teen, doesn't seem to bother Buttermaker (or the filmmakers).

Naturally, the Bears begin winning as things go from outlandishly bad to Leak hitting balls out of the park and Amanda striking out tons of hitters.

As the games get ugly and the unmitigated zeal about demolishing the opponent infiltrates the Bears and the Yankees, Ritchie hits a hilarious grand slam against all that can ruin Little League.

Classic Scene: After a heartbreaking loss in the championship game, 7-6 to the Yankees, Buttermaker knows how to make his team feel better.

He lets them invade his beer cooler.

At the awards presentation, as the Yankees tote their huge first-place trophy and Buttermaker is given a puny second-place keepsake, the winners credit the Bears for their "guts," while still saying they aren't very good. Toilet-mouthed Boyle then tells them where to shove their trophy, and the Bears proceed to dump beer all over each other in celebration as if they'd won.

Classic Line: Buttermaker's best verbal sparring comes against Amanda, of whom he clearly is protective. From trying to convince her to join the squad to trying to prevent her from growing up, his exchanges with her are dead-on.

> Buttermaker: "Those boys aren't very rough. You won't get hurt."
>
> Amanda: "That's got nothing to do with it. I'm almost 12 and I'll . . . I'll be getting a bra soon." [Buttermaker stares at her and Amanda then looks at her chest.]
>
> Amanda: "Well, maybe in a year or so. I can't be playing all dumb baseball."
>
> And when Amanda tells Buttermaker she is going on a date:
>
> Buttermaker: "What if he tries something?"

Amanda: "I'll handle it."

Buttermaker: "Rolling Stones, 11 years old."

Amanda: "I know an 11-year-old girl who is already on the pill."

Buttermaker: "Don't ever say that word again."

Amanda: "Jesus! Just who in the heck you think you are?"

Buttermaker: "The goddamned manager, that's who!"

KINGPIN

The Farrelly Brothers have shown no hesitation about rolling over anyone for a laugh. So when they turned to the bowling alleys of America to make *Kingpin*, well, they threw a lot of strikes.

And, as in any sports comedy, they put a few in the gutter, too.

Bowling is one of America's favorite pastimes as a participant sport. It's not quite up there with the NFL on television, with its heyday on TV having occurred decades ago when the likes of Dick Weber, Don Carter, Carmen Salvino, and Earl Anthony were stars.

Keglers haven't gotten much attention in the movies, either. Which made them and their sport ripe for the Farrellys.

The brothers collected Bill Murray, Randy Quaid, Woody Harrelson, Chris Elliott, and a bunch of others in 1996, shooting for that 300 game. Along the way, they came up with some 7-10 splits, but also hit their marks with jocular regularity.

Roy Munson (Harrelson, in one of his goofiest roles) was destined to become Kingpin until his right hand was cut off when he and another rising star of the alleys, Ernie McCracken (Murray), hustle some locals.

Munson becomes a salesman, but he can't get rid of the bowling bug. When he meets Ishmael (Quaid), an Amish man—yes, the Farrellys go there, too, with good game—Munson talks Ishmael into joining him on the road as trainer/manager and bowler. They will get rich through bowling and save Ishmael's farm from foreclosure, too.

Ishmael, who had to sneak away from his farm and family to surreptitiously bowl, takes to the world away from that lifestyle very quickly, although he does go catatonic during a car chase.

Turns out Ishmael's game wasn't so strong, and he often used 15 frames to post his scores, adhering to an Amish tradition of "half again." But Munson is a good teacher and soon they are rolling along, ready to take on the very best in the sport: McCracken.

Murray is in total over-the-top mode as McCracken. When he meets up with Munson and Ishmael, it isn't quite a lovefest, and Ishmael belies his peace-loving roots once more, taking a swing at McCracken. He connects—with a wall.

Broken hand, no million-dollar payday on the horizon.

Unless, as Ishmael suggests, Munson can overcome his demons and his disability and enter the big-money tournament himself.

Which he does, leading to a series of unlikely victories. Although he loses the final to the repulsive McCracken, he strikes an endorsement deal with Trojan condoms because Roy now has earned the nickname "Rubber Man."

Yes, the Farrellys go there, as well.

Classic Scene: "Let's Start the Tournament," the announcer yells, and lane after lane of bowlers approach the foul line and throw their ball. Only Munson stands back, frozen with fear. He turns to Ishmael and mouths "I can't." But Ishmael, holding up a sign saying "Go Roy" (the other side says "Will Work for Food") nods in encouragement, and Munson reluctantly turns toward the pins.

His approach is perfect, but as he releases the ball, down the lane goes his prosthetic hand, the fingers stuck in the holes of the ball. Munson does a double-take, then looks at his hook as the ball and fake hand reach the pocket—and knock down all 10 pins, to loud cheers and looks of amazement.

Munson walks back to the ball return and asks his fellow bowler: "You wouldn't happen to have a Phillips-head screwdriver, would you?"

Then the ball, with hand still attached, comes back through the ball return.

"Never mind," Munson says with a sigh of relief.

Classic Line: With a tournament on the line, no one could be more obnoxious than Ernie McCracken. Anything for an edge.

So as Munson prepares to bowl:

McCracken: "It all comes down to this roll. Roy Munson, a man-child with a dream to topple bowling giant Ernie

McCracken. If he strikes, he's the 1979 Odor-Eaters Champion. He's got one foot in the frying pan and one in the pressure cooker. Believe me, as a bowler, I know that right about now, your bladder feels like an overstuffed vacuum cleaner bag, and your butt is kind of like an about-to-explode bratwurst."

Munson: "Hey, do you mind? I wasn't talking when you were bowling."

McCracken: "Was I talking out loud? Was I? Sorry. Good luck."

DODGEBALL: A TRUE UNDERDOG STORY

Any film that can team Ben Stiller, Vince Vaughn, and a slew of comedic character actors ranging from Rip Torn to Gary Cole, then throw in Chuck Norris and Lance Armstrong appearing as themselves almost guarantees yuks.

Build the plot around the most niche of sports—games, really—and you have Crazyball meets *Dodgeball*.

Plots rarely mean much in Stiller/Vaughn films, and the one here is pretty basic.

White Goodman (Stiller) owns Globo Gym and desires to take over the gym market in his area. Only one thing stands in his way: the Average Joe's gym, run by Peter LaFleur (Vaughn).

Average Joe's is a less-than-average gym with a cast of characters most establishments, seedy or not, wouldn't welcome.

Eventually and inevitably, Goodman's planned takeover comes down to the gritty basics, the place where Stiller, complete with a wicked Fu Manchu, and Vaughn operate best: absurd comedy.

A pretty much winner-take-all dodgeball match is arranged between the Average Joes and the Globo Gym Purple Cobras.

LaFleur's group of misfits has no chance of winning to keep the gym in his hands until the legend of the dodgeball arena, Patches O'Houlihan (Torn), takes on the challenge of whipping these losers into a team worthy of even playing the sport.

Until they get after each other on the court, Stiller and Vaughn often take a backseat to some of the eccentric characters populating this farce: the nerd who dreams of bedding the oh-so-hot cheerleader; the guy who knows everything about any sport you barely have heard of and care even less about; and, if you will, a 21st-century pirate on the lookout for buried treasure (great comedic turn by Alan Tudyk).

Will good—well, mediocre—triumph over evil? A better question might be, will dodgeball become an Olympic sport?

Classic Scene: If you can dodge . . .

The wheelchair-riding O'Houlihan's training of the Average Joes features anything-but-average techniques.

As he gathers the prospective players together, he dumps a bag filled with tools on the floor of the gym.

"If you can dodge a wrench, you can dodge a ball," he declares, then he chucks the wrench at one of the Joes, conking him on the noggin and knocking him over.

Then they hit the streets, because, "If you can dodge traffic, you can dodge a ball."

Moments later, another of the Joes gets crunched by a car. Twice.

How else would you build a winning team?

Classic Line: Peter, meet Lance.

Lance, meet Peter.

Armstrong: "Could I get a bottle of water? Hey, aren't you Peter La Fleur?"

La Fleur: "Lance Armstrong!"

Armstrong: "Yeah, that's me. But I'm a big fan of yours."

La Fleur: "Really?"

Armstrong: "Yeah, I've been watching the dodgeball tournament on the Ocho. ESPN 8. I just can't get enough of it. Good luck in the tournament. I'm really pulling for you against those jerks from Globo Gym. I think you better hurry up or you're gonna be late."

La Fleur: "Uh, actually I decided to quit."

Armstrong: "Quit? You know, once I was thinking about quitting when I was diagnosed with brain, lung, and testicular cancer, all at the same time. But with the love and support of my friends and family, I got back on the bike and I won the Tour de France five times in a row. But I'm sure you have a good reason to quit.So what are you dying from that's keeping you from the finals?"

La Fleur: "Right now it feels a little bit like shame."

Armstrong: "Well, I guess if a person never quit when the going got tough, they wouldn't have anything to regret for the rest of their life. But good luck to you, Peter. I'm sure this decision won't haunt you forever."

7

WHAT WERE THEY THINKING?

Trading a future Hall of Famer is tough enough. Getting back guys who will only get into the Hall of Fame if they pay their admission at the door or get hired as ushers at the shrine is a million times worse.

Yet every major sport has its "What were they thinking?" transactions. Here are a dirty dozen steals, uh, deals, that paid huge dividends for one side and tore apart the other. Call it Crazyball in the front office.

BASEBALL

In no sport is bartering players more ingrained than in baseball. Even now, in the days of guaranteed contracts and role players—particularly pitchers—the megadeal is magic.

Here are five trades that were pure gold on one side, tarnished tin on the other.

Babe Ruth, Red Sox to Yankees

No debating this one. Ruth was the catalyst for the Yankees becoming U.S. sports' most successful franchise. The trade was only the beginning of unwise maneuvers on and off the field by the Red Sox, who became a laughingstock through the decades for dealing away the greatest player in baseball history.

In 1920, Boston already had won five World Series and was among the elite teams playing America's pastime. The Yankees had all of zero championships.

But Red Sox owner Harry Frazee was desperate for cash and had no strong feelings for Beantown, either, once saying, "The best thing about Boston was the train ride back to New York."

His pet project was launching a Broadway musical, *No, No, Nanette*—Frazee made his money as a producer of shows, also losing money on them and with a gambling habit. His best asset in Boston was Ruth.

Technically, because there were no players heading to Boston, it was a straight sale when Frazee handed over the slugger (and, for several years, front-line pitcher) to New York for $125,000 and a $300,000 loan.

No, No, Nanette was a mild hit in Manhattan. Ruth was a slightly bigger hit in the Bronx.

And the "Curse of the Bambino" lasted for more than 80 years, as the Red Sox repeatedly failed to win another World Series until 2004.

Frank Robinson, Reds to Orioles

Outfielder Robinson was one of the most versatile players in baseball, a hard hitter, good fielder with a strong arm. In 1961, Robinson had one of the most productive years in history, winning the Triple Crown with 49 home runs, 122 RBIs, and a .316 batting average. Cincinnati lost to the Yankees in the World Series, the first time the Reds got that far since 1940.

Four years later, Reds general manager Bill DeWitt decided that the 30-year-old Robinson was on the downside of his career. He sent Robby to the Baltimore Orioles for pitchers Milt Pappas and Jack Baldschun and outfielder Dick Simpson.

At least he got quality in return, but not nearly what Robinson delivered in the American League. Robby led the Orioles to four World Series in six seasons in Baltimore, winning twice. He was a unanimous league MVP in 1966, and entered the Hall of Fame in 1982.

This trade was lopsided enough that it earned a mention in the film *Bull Durham*.

"But bad trades are part of baseball," said Annie Savoy (Susan Sarandon). "Now who can forget Frank Robinson for Milt Pappas, for God's sake?"

Nolan Ryan, Mets to Angels

Those laughable Mets, who redefined Crazyball with manager Casey Stengel's double-talk and their skill at hitting into double (and triple) plays, had stepped away from their clown show days by 1971. Heck, they'd won a World Series in '69, and had built the best young pitching staff in the majors.

It was so deep and so good, in fact, that the Mets decided they could trade away the most undisciplined—if strongest—arm: a right-hander named Nolan Ryan.

Ryan was raw—so were his fingers, which he often soaked in pickle brine to harden—and wild, with a 29-38 record and a ton of walks (344) to go with a ton of strikeouts (493). The Mets lost patience, and with a hole at third base, they sent Ryan to the California Angels for Jim Fregosi, an accomplished shortstop who would be moved over to third base.

Fregosi flopped in the Big Apple. The "Ryan Express" blossomed in Southern California, and soon was the most powerful and feared pitcher in baseball. He lasted only until he was 46 years old, finishing off a Hall of Fame career with 324 wins, seven no-hitters, and an unfathomable—and possibly unapproachable—5,714 strikeouts.

"Ryan is the only guy who puts fear in me," Reggie Jackson once said. "Not because he can get you out, but because he can kill you."

Roger Maris, Athletics to Yankees

The joke used to be that Kansas City was part of the Yankees' farm system, even though the Athletics were in the American League. The way the Yankees pilfered the A's was no laughing matter, though.

And the biggest joke of all was KC sending right fielder Roger Maris to the Bronx Bombers—where he became, at least for one season, the greatest Bomber of them all.

The aloof, sometimes acerbic Maris at his core was a shy man from the Midwest. He fit perfectly in Kansas City, but New York could be a bit overwhelming for him, especially performing in the shadow of the bon vivant center fielder Mickey Mantle, the most popular Yankee of all in 1960 when the deal was completed.

But Maris fit perfectly in the Yankees' lineup, making Mantle and other such stars as Yogi Berra, Bill Skowron, and Elston Howard even more dangerous. He was the American League MVP in his first season in pinstripes, and again the next year, 1961. That's when the M&M boys set after Babe Ruth's record 60 homers in one season. Maris got there first with 61—with an asterisk, of course, in the record books, because he did it in a 162-game season and Ruth in 154.

Yet because he was not Mantle, New Yorkers and many others in and out of baseball were not enamored of Maris's feat.

It made Maris bitter.

"Now they talk on the radio about the record set by Ruth, and DiMaggio and Henry Aaron," Maris said years later. "But they rarely mention mine. Do you know what I have to show for the 61 home runs? Nothing, exactly nothing."

Which pretty much was what Kansas City had to show for dealing away Maris. The A's were more like Z's. Although the three men they acquired—Hank Bauer, Norm Siebern, and the only man to throw a no-hitter (perfect game, actually) in the World Series, Don Larsen—were solid players, Kansas City never won more than 74 games in a season after the deal before moving to Oakland in 1968.

Lou Brock, Cubs to Cardinals

Ernie Broglio was the winningest pitcher in baseball in 1960, going 21-9 for the St. Louis Cardinals. He won 18 games in

1963 with five shutouts. The Chicago Cubs believed they needed to solidify their staff and that Broglio, at 28, had plenty of life left in his right arm.

Lou Brock was a middling hitter and decent fielder who showed little at the plate for Chicago in parts of three seasons, and wasn't doing much in 1964. At the trade deadline, June 15, the Cubs sent him to the Cards in a six-player deal.

Pardon the pun, but it was quite the steal for St. Loo.

Brock hit .348 as a Cardinal in 1964 and the team won the World Series. From there, Brock really took off—literally. He led the National League in stolen bases eight times, hit .300 seven times, won another championship in 1967, and sped into Cooperstown as the all-time steals leader (since surpassed by Rickey Henderson).

"Lou Brock, along with Maury Wills, are probably the two players most responsible for the biggest change in the game over the last 15 years," Hall of Fame pitcher Tom Seaver said in 1987.

Broglio? The main man in the six-player deal for the Cubs won a total of four games for Chicago.

BASKETBALL

Robert Parish and Rights to Kevin McHale, Warriors to Celtics

How desperate were the Golden State Warriors to get center Joe Barry Carroll on their roster? Enough to trade away two future Hall of Famers.

Carroll was the top player available in the 1980 NBA draft, a defensive force from Purdue who also could score, rebound, and cause havoc in the paint. The Warriors saw him as the perfect antidote to the likes of Kareem Abdul-Jabbar, then the pre-eminent center in basketball.

Boston, whose dynasty was still flourishing as the most successful franchise in basketball history, had just added Larry Bird to its lineup. With the third overall selection, acquired in the deal, general manager Red Auerbach picked Kevin McHale of Minnesota. Golden State also sent its starting center, Robert Parish, to Beantown, and got back the No. 13 overall pick, which it used for guard Rickey Brown of Mississippi State.

Always considered a coaching genius, Auerbach had built a reputation as a smart GM and personnel guy. After this trade, he could have been looked upon as a thief.

The 6-10 McHale went on to define the position of power forward. Teaming with the 6-9 Bird, who could do anything, and the 7-0 Parish, the Celtics were long, rugged, and versatile.

Boston won three NBA titles and made the finals five times with that trio as its core. Bird, Parish, and McHale were voted to the NBA's 50 Greatest Players list.

Carroll? He was a pretty decent player, but never a difference-maker in his decade in the NBA.

New York Daily News columnist Filip Bondy compared Auerbach's fleecing of the Warriors to the work of Peter Minuit.

"The Dutch colonial governor edges out Red Auerbach and Napoleon," Bondy wrote. "Auerbach may have traded Joe Barry Carroll for Robert Parish and the rights to draft

Kevin McHale, but Minuit exchanged $24 worth of trinkets in 1626 for the island of Manhattan."

Auerbach was plenty happy with his steal of a deal.

Julius Erving, Nets to 76ers

When the New York Nets joined the NBA following the folding of the ABA in 1976, Nets owner Roy Boe couldn't meet the payments to keep his team alive. He owed $8 million—$3.2 million to the NBA and $4.8 million to the Knicks as compensation for allowing the Nets to play in the same territory, at the time Long Island.

He had one asset that was worth enough to keep the Nets from disappearing: Julius Erving.

So Boe did his best Harry Frazee imitation, selling Dr. J to the Philadelphia 76ers for $3 million. The transaction robbed the franchise of any chance of being competitive—for years.

It so enraged Nets fans that a group of season ticket holders sued Boe and got their money back. The team soon would move to New Jersey, but hardly anyone noticed, with Dr. J working his magic in Philadelphia.

And what magic that was, as the game's most exciting player, a soaring, dunking, finger-rolling wizard who alone was worth the price of admission.

The Sixers regularly sold out and contended, making four finals and winning the NBA championship in 1983. Erving was the league's biggest attraction until Magic Johnson, Larry Bird, and Michael Jordan came along.

Years later, Boe spoke about the "Curse of Dr. J."

"I don't call that a curse, I call it bad luck," he said of the Nets' string of, well, bad luck. "But, you know, there are others who feel differently."

Kareem Abdul-Jabbar, Bucks to Lakers
Kobe Bryant, Hornets to Lakers

We'll lump these two together under Lakers Larceny.

Kareem Abdul-Jabbar always has been a winner, whether as the most unstoppable force in high school at Power Memorial in New York City or while at UCLA, where he led the Bruins to three NCAA crowns in as many years as Lew Alcindor.

He was the NBA's top draft pick in 1969 when the Milwaukee Bucks won a coin flip with the Phoenix Suns, and in his second season, he carried the Bucks to the championship as Abdul-Jabbar.

Yet by 1975, with no more championship notches on his belt, Abdul-Jabbar wanted out of Milwaukee. It was for cultural reasons as much as a basketball consideration: Abdul-Jabbar, a roundball renaissance man, felt stifled in Wisconsin.

Behind-the-scenes negotiations with Bucks management led to talks with other teams, including Alcindor's hometown Knicks, although the Knicks never really were in the race because the Knicks basically wanted to buy Abdul-Jabbar rather than trade for him.

Atlanta was next to bid, but quickly the Bucks turned their attention west. Wisely, the Lakers were very interested.

When the deal went down, Milwaukee got four good players in center Elmore Smith to step in for Abdul-Jabbar;

swingman Junior Bridgeman; guard Brian Winters; and forward Dave Meyers. All four had been stars in college and would be impressive enough pros.

Abdul-Jabbar became the sport's all-time scoring leader with 37,387 points, many on his unblockable sky hook that was as much a signature weapon as Bobby Hull's slapshot or Nolan Ryan's fastball.

With the Lakers, Abdul-Jabbar won five rings. With the Bucks, the quartet of players obtained for the 7-2 pivotman never reached the NBA finals.

Oh, the Bucks did get some money from the Lakers. As Bucks general manager Wayne Embry told the *New York Post*: "How much? I'm ashamed to admit, something like $250,000."

LA was at it again in 1996 when the teenage son of former pro Joe Bryant became eligible for the draft out of high school. Unlike his dad, who was a backup forward and center for much of his eight-year NBA career, Kobe Bryant was a shooting guard with immeasurable potential.

The Charlotte Hornets seemed to recognize that, selecting Kobe with the 13th pick. Then they went brain-dead, dealing him to the Lakers for center Vlade Divac. The 7-1 Divac might have been best known for flopping on the court to draw charges.

Or was that how it happened? Members of the Hornets' front office always have claimed that the deal was completed before the draft, with the Lakers actually making the 13th pick and taking Bryant.

"The deal was actually done a day ahead of time, and it was Vlade for a player to be named," Bill Branch, the Hornets' head scout at the time, told the *Winston-Salem Journal*.

"If I remember right, they didn't even tell us who they wanted us to pick until about five minutes before the pick was made. So it was never a matter of us actually drafting Kobe."

Not that it really matters; would Charlotte (or any other team, for that matter) do it again?

Bryant, who lived in Europe when his father was playing there but attended high school in a Philadelphia suburb, eventually teamed with a slightly more accomplished center than Divac: Shaquille O'Neal. Together, they won three championships with the Lakers, then Bryant led his team to two more titles without Shaq.

The serviceable Divac lasted only two seasons in Charlotte. There are no championship rings on his fingers.

HOCKEY

Guy Lafleur, Seals to Canadiens

Everyone knew long before he became eligible for the NHL draft that Guy Lafleur would be the No. 1 overall pick in 1971 and would help some fortunate franchise rise toward the top.

Everyone, apparently, except the Oakland Seals.

And the lucky recipients of the Seals' ignorance? None other than hockey's most successful team, the Montreal Canadiens.

For decades, the best French-Canadian players wound up with Montreal, in part because of a territorial draft rule that no longer was in existence by the 1970s. Indeed, Gilbert

Perreault was the hands-down top prospect in 1970 and he went to Buffalo.

So the Canadiens, who had won the Stanley Cup in 1968 and '69, had little hope of seeing "The Flower" don the bleu, blanc, and rouge.

But they could try, and in May 1970, their brilliant general manager, Sam Pollock, persuaded Seals owner Charles O. Finley—yes, the same guy who owned baseball's A's and made them into a champion and a laughingstock at various times—to take young forward Ernie Hicke and the Canadiens' first-round choice that year, Chris Oddliefson. Montreal got back defenseman François Lacombe—and the Seals' first-round pick in 1971.

But Pollock wasn't through. Realizing that another California team, the Kings, could fall into the basement, Pollock traded one of his better players, center Ralph Backstrom, to Los Angeles in hopes that Backstrom's leadership and talents could boost the Kings over the Seals.

Mission accomplished.

Just weeks after winning yet another Stanley Cup, the Canadiens grabbed Lafleur in the draft. Pollock's smile lit up the Queen Elizabeth Hotel—in Montreal, no less.

While the Seals, renamed the California Golden Seals that year, when they actually wore white skates with their gold uniforms, remained floppers, Lafleur led the Canadiens to five Stanley Cups, including all four from 1976–1979 as hockey's best player. Helmetless, with a tremendous burst of speed, a deadly shot, and a flair for the dramatic, Lafleur was recognized as the most dynamic force in hockey in that decade.

Oakland lost its hockey team in 1976 to Cleveland, where the renamed Barons folded after two seasons.

And Pollock never lost that Cheshire Cat smile.

"It was," he once said in over-the-top understatement, "a pretty good trade."

8

SPORTS AS THEATER

SEEING RED

Everyone knows the Harlem Globetrotters. But how about those All-American Red Heads?

Like the Globetrotters, the Red Heads enjoyed widespread popularity as a barnstorming basketball team.

Like the Globetrotters, the Red Heads mixed in clowning with their brilliant basketball skills.

Like the Globetrotters, the Red Heads usually won their games.

One big difference—the Red Heads was an all-girls team.

They usually played only men's teams, under men's rules.

For 50 years, the Red Heads took on all comers as they traveled around North America and beyond, playing some 200 games a season from fall to spring. Once pointing out the differences between the Red Heads and Globetrotters, owner Orwell Moore said, "The Globetrotters bring their own opponents along. We don't know who we're going to play from night to night."

While the Globetrotters played their perennial whipping boys, the Washington Generals, the Red Heads took on opponents from American Legion posts, Lions Club teams, Indian reservations, and military bases, not to mention players from pro football teams. Despite all the fooling around, most of the time the Red Heads were practically unbeatable. Their roster was filled with some of the best women's basketball talent in America.

It had started as a publicity stunt.

In 1936, C. M. Olsen had an idea to promote his wife's beauty salon: What if a girls' basketball team were all redheads?

Olsen formed a team that became extremely popular. Some of the players were natural redheads; others dyed their hair.

Carolyn Booth played in 1966-67. For her, the Red Heads were "a growing up year for me."

"The first thing I remember is that I had to dye my hair red. I was the last one in the group to do so. I took a little ragging."

That practice continued through generations of "redheads" from 1936–1986. Along the way, the franchise was sold to Orville Moore of Caraway, Arkansas, in 1955.

The Red Heads are generally regarded as the first women's professional basketball team in America.

Brenda Koester, for one, played in over 640 games for the Red Heads in three years, 1970–1973. In that time she scored over 10,000 points.

"Our record in 1972-73 was 199 wins and 6 losses. We won 96 games in a row," she proudly boasts.

That left little time for sleeping.

Another memory: traveling all night, crowded into an old station wagon.

"Sometimes we would have to practice after a game and travel all night to another location to play a game. Sleep was something we didn't get too much of on those occasions. We looked like a bunch of convicts, except we didn't have shovels and slings."

They did have roadwork. Moore made sure of it, particularly on the rare nights that the Red Heads lost.

Winning produced a different reaction. Yodeling.

"If he was happy and we were winning games, he would come and visit us—we would sing and he would yodel."

Wearing red, white, and blue uniforms, the Red Heads were a mix of fun and serious basketball. They advertised themselves as the "World's Champion Girls' Basketball Team." They blazed a trail for women's basketball, long before it became popular in the '70s and '80s.

Moore imported only the best female basketball talent in America.

Mickey Childress was typical of the kind of talent he signed for the Red Heads. She was a standout high school center in Virginia who set a state record of 81 points in one game before playing at the University of Tennessee.

"A lot of times, the men came in expecting a bunch of girls they could push around," said Childress, who played in the early 1960s. "But we were in condition. Our first quarter was pure basketball. We wanted to show the public that we knew how to first of all play basketball."

The rest, pure entertainment.

Whether playing in gymnasiums in small towns or big city arenas, the Red Heads usually packed them in with their frantic, fun-filled antics. Once establishing their serious basketball talents, it was showtime. The show also featured halftime activities such as trick shooting, dribbling, and juggling.

"Each girl had her own specialty," Childress said. "Mine was the head shot."

Childress bounced the ball into the net off her head.

Another favorite: the "Old Piggy Back Play." A player climbed on the shoulders of another. On to the basket. Score!

Then there was the "Pinch Play." Referees were in on the prank.

A Red Head would stop the action with a shout, "He pinched me!" She pointed to an astounded player on the opposing team.

"I'd try to choose the most bashful guy on the floor," Childress said.

"Foul!" the referee declared. A Red Head was given two free throws—shot from her knees.

The referee would then get a kiss on the top of his head with an overload of lipstick from a Red Head—particularly if he was short and balding.

The crowd loved it!

Moore said the Globetrotters actually stole some of the Red Heads' routines, including the Piggy Back routine, the Referee Act, and the La Conga Out of Bounds act.

Thirteen years after the franchise folded, the Red Heads were enshrined in the Naismith Memorial Basketball Hall of Fame for their contribution in developing women's basketball in America. They were the first female basketball team to be so honored.

"We liked to think we helped women's basketball to stay alive when the colleges weren't playing our game," Childress said.

HAIL CESAR

It didn't happen often, but at least once the All-American Red Heads had a hard time getting their heads into a game. It was on a stop in Hollywood when they met movie star Cesar Romero, one of the leading romantic actors of his day.

"He sat right on the bench with us," said Hazel Cone, who played for the Red Heads in the 1930s. "He cheered us and hugged us and patted our shoulders whenever we scored."

As a matter of practice two girls had to take their turn sitting out games, but that night none of the Red Heads minded being stuck on the bench.

"We all took turns sitting out for the opportunity to sit with Cesar."

Cone said she didn't remember if the Red Heads won or lost, "but we had the best time ever."

STOP THAT GIRL!

The All-American Red Heads liked to have fun, but then came a time for serious basketball.

"A team ran a woman on the court against us and Coach Moore was looking around and telling us how necessary and important it was that she not score a single point," said Linda Kidd, who played for the Red Heads in 1966 and 1967.

Moore also emphasized how intense the roadwork was going to be for the person who let her score.

"We know he meant it; besides, all of us took it seriously that we could outplay anyone who challenged us on the court."

Then Moore looked at Kidd.

"He said, 'She's your man.' I was exhilarated. Jolene [Moore] looked at me and the rest of the girls and simply said, 'OK, let's go.'"

"Her confidence in my being able to hold that player is something I will never forget."

With the rest of the team's help, that lady went home that night without scoring a point.

"Pretty hard to score if you cannot get your hands on the ball."

HALL OF FAME VEHICLE

When the Women's Basketball Hall of Fame opened in Knoxville, Tennessee, in 1999, an old station wagon took center stage. It brought back memories.

The wagon was actually used by one of the many teams representing the All-American Red Heads in their travels around the country.

The rusted old wagon had been sitting, a pile of junk in a field, when it was discovered in the late '90s. Orwell Moore still owned the rights to the vehicle, a 24-foot 1966 Pontiac Catalina.

"It was nasty," said Jeff Simpson, director of marketing for the Knoxville Sports Corp., which purchased the vehicle for the Hall of Fame museum. "There were snake skins and mice in it, and the axle was so rusted that the whole car had to be scooped up and placed on a flatbed truck."

Moore originally wanted $20,000 for the vehicle, but settled for $500. It took a major restoration job to return the wagon to its former glory.

"It will help tell a good story," said Gloria Ray, president and chief executive officer of the Knoxville Sports Corp. "Today, women's professional basketball teams fly around the country. In their day, the Red Heads drove around the country in this car."

ANOTHER RED HEAD

"I'm the losingest coach in the world, but I won't get fired," said Red Klotz, longtime owner/coach of the Washington Generals. "Pretty amazing, huh?"

Not when you know the Generals. Losing was their job.

For a major part of the Harlem Globetrotters' existence, the Generals were their comic foils. In these fun-filled exhibitions, the Generals played straight men to the Globetrotters' clowns.

The fix was in. The Generals played it straightforward with traditional layups, jump shots, and man-to-man defense while the Globetrotters did their thing: bouncing basketballs off each other's butts, chasing each other into the stands with buckets of confetti, and pretending to shoot free throws, then laughing as the Generals jumped for rebounds that never existed.

The rules of the game were suspended as far as the Globetrotters were concerned, anyway. They could do anything they wanted to the hapless Generals, including pulling down their shorts and sticking basketballs in the back of their jerseys.

"We play with a sense of humor and an understanding of what this is all about," said Klotz of the Generals' role in this long-running comic melodrama.

The script always ended with the Globetrotters winning.

Well, almost always.

Crazyball hit on January 5, 1971. The scene was a modest little gym in Martin, Tennessee. Then 50, the 5-foot-7 Klotz still possessed some of the skills that made him one of the best long-range shooters in the NBA in the 1940s.

The teams were playing out their usual script, the Globetrotters about to finish off another victory over the Generals, this time playing under the disguise of the New Jersey Reds.

Then something unusual happened: Klotz, forgetting his role as loser, swished a long-range shot to push the Reds into the lead.

There was still enough time for the Globetrotters to pull out a victory. The ball was in Meadowlark Lemon's hands. But Lemon, one of the most popular players in Globetrotters history, missed the shot.

New Jersey Reds 100, Harlem Globetrotters 99.

That ended a winning streak for the Globetrotters over their "rivals" that had extended through 2,495 games.

For a while, there was silence in the arena. Then boos, as the Reds left the court. Kids were crying.

"They weren't pleased at all," Klotz said. "They reacted like we had just killed Santa Claus."

In the dressing room, the Reds celebrated, spraying soda on one another. No wonder. It was only the sixth time the Globetrotters had been beaten in this fast-breaking traveling show, and would be the last time before Klotz "retired" the Generals' identity in 1995. In the 40-plus years of their association, the Globetrotters beat the Generals more than 13,000 times, according to Klotz.

It was a relationship that started in 1953, when Globetrotters owner Abe Saperstein invited Klotz to join him as a professional victim.

"He said, 'I want you to get a good team together to play us every night,'" Klotz remembered of Saperstein's offer. "I said, 'I'm going to beat you.' And he said, 'You're going to try.'"

Klotz wasn't used to losing games. As a member of the American Basketball League's Philadelphia Sphas in the 1940s, Klotz's team had actually beaten the Globetrotters in an exhibition game, not to mention other good teams.

Klotz was a product of Philadelphia. He had led South Philadelphia High School to the city championship and played for Villanova before helping the Baltimore Bullets win the NBA championship in 1948.

It was a different game with the Generals, who had to be good actors as well as good basketball players. Example: When the Globetrotters went into their popular football sketch, lining up on the court as if in an NFL game, the Generals feigned surprise.

"Being a good General means first off being a good basketball player," Klotz said. "If I put a bunch of stiffs out there, the crowd would hate it. Our guys have to have enough talent to make a ballgame out of things every night."

To fill the Generals' roster, Klotz went after players in the college ranks, just like the NBA. These players knew they weren't going to be another Michael Jordan, or even play in the NBA at all. They were professionals, nevertheless, as they followed the Globetrotters to distant exotic places around the world. They played a staggering 250 games in a 12-month cycle. And they played under a host of other names as well: the Boston Shamrocks, Baltimore Rockets, Atlantic City Seagulls, New Jersey Reds, and New York Nationals. After "retiring" the Generals, Klotz brought them back to life for a brief period in the '90s.

The Generals lasted the longest and were the opponents most recognized as the Globetrotters' main foil.

To paraphrase Vince Lombardi, as far as Klotz was concerned: losing wasn't everything, it was the only thing.

CLOSE CALL

It was the early 1950s when Klotz took the Generals on a trip abroad to play the Globetrotters before the Shah of Iran. At first Klotz wondered if it was a good idea.

"He had survived about 100 attempts on his life, so everybody was a little jumpy," Klotz recalled.

When the Generals got to the court, Klotz realized that he had forgotten the basketballs. He ran back toward the bus to get them. Suddenly a bloodcurdling scream rang out, and a guard jammed a gun barrel in Klotz's stomach.

"If I hadn't stopped, the guy would have turned me into Swiss cheese," Klotz told *Sports Illustrated* in a 1995 interview. "It was a scary moment."

Really? When he looked back, Klotz saw all his players giggling hysterically.

"I'm afraid we lost the game, but I had to look on the bright side . . . nobody died."

ROAD WARRIORS

One of Klotz's favorite road stories featured a tour he made to the Middle East in 1953.

The Generals had just lost another game to the Globetrotters, this time in Syria. The teams were all set to take off for Istanbul when it was discovered the plane was overweight.

Saperstein, the Globetrotters' owner, ordered Klotz and four players off the plane. The party of five was forced to drive 100 miles to Beirut to pick up another flight.

"I stopped at the Lebanese border and everybody is running around like crazy with machine guns, getting ready to go to war with Israel for the umpteenth time," Klotz said in an interview with *Sports Illustrated*.

Klotz pulled out his passport. That's when the trouble started.

"I'm trying to identify myself by pretending to dribble and shoot, but the guards just keep looking at my visa list that had 42 names on it, and they want to know where we've buried the bodies of the other 37 guys. It didn't help much that the first two names on the list were Saperstein and Klotz."

Happy ending. Klotz's persistence finally paid off and his Generals were on their way to another loss to the Globetrotters.

9

CRAZY SUPERSTITIONS, CRAZY FANS, AND OTHER LOCKER ROOM TALES

TURK'S QUIRKS

In the 1998 movie *Bull Durham*, the character Annie Savoy, played by Susan Sarandon, persuades Nuke LaLoosh to wear a garter belt under his uniform while pitching.

It was not so far-fetched, considering the wildly superstitious nature of baseball players. That type of behavior has been going on as far back as anyone can remember.

Take George Stallings, manager of the 1914 Miracle Braves. Superstition was a big part of Stallings's managing style.

"If he was caught leaning over picking up a pebble in the coach's box at third base and the light-hitting Braves started a rally, George would freeze in a stance that was almost catatonic until the rally was over," said one newspaperman.

One hundred years later, not much has changed in the area of baseball superstition.

Wade Boggs, for instance, ate chicken before every game he played. Reliever Turk Wendell chewed black licorice while pitching, brushing his teeth between innings. Jason Giambi wore a gold lamé thong to help him break out of a slump. He even loaned it to teammates who needed a few hits. Who cared if it worked or not? That didn't faze Giambi.

Wendell, who pitched for the Chicago Cubs, New York Mets, Philadelphia Phillies, and Colorado Rockies, was cited by one national magazine as the most superstitious athlete of all time.

Just some of Turk's quirks:

- Whenever his catcher stood, Wendell would crouch down.
- Whenever he began a new inning, Wendell would turn and wave to the center fielder.
- Wendell insisted that the umpire roll the ball to the mound rather than simply throw it to him.

Wendell also was fascinated by the number 9 for some reason, working it into the number he wore on his uniform and even one of the contracts he signed: $9,999,999.99.

"It's such a hard game," broadcaster Jon Miller told the *San Jose Mercury News*. "It's just a given that you're going to have a bad day, a tough week, a horrible month. So when guys are going bad, stuff like this is a way for players to make sure it doesn't ruin your life. It keeps you stable."

SUPERSTITIOUS, BY GEORGE

While baseball players are known to be a superstitious lot, former Denver Nuggets coach George Karl could give them a pretty good run for their money, literally. Reported *USA Today*: Karl has made it a practice to touch the head of every player before they go on the court. He takes all the money out of his pocket and puts it in a pouch strapped to his ankle. He never wears the same tie two days in a row and if his team loses, he doesn't wear the same tie for a month. And he won't sit on the bench until after tip-off.

Karl explained why he can't let go of his superstitions: "You think of them when you are miserable after a loss and talking to the gods at 4:00 a.m. in your hotel room."

SUPERSTITIOUS GODS?

When it comes to superstitions, Canadian racetrack trainers take a backseat to no one.

"You have to have skill and talent to win a horse race," said race track veteran Jared Brown, "but at least half is probably luck. So why anger the racing gods?"

Some of Brown's superstitions:

- When a horse is in the paddock and you take the halter off, you can never let it hit the ground.
- Pitchforks have to be kept completely clean—not a shred of straw clinging to the metal.
- And never hang a horseshoe upside down.

Brown, a longtime trainer at Assiniboia Downs, made his views known in an interview with the *Winnipeg Free Press*. Calling on the racing deities must be working for him at least some of the time. Brown has trained over 2,200 horses and finished first 281 times.

NAILING IT DOWN

"Concrete Charlie,""Hammer," and "Nails."

Those are only some of the colorful nicknames applied through the years by Philadelphia sports fans to their most popular athletes.

Concrete Charlie was Eagles football star Chuck Bednarik, Hammer was the Flyers' hard hitter Dave Schultz, and Nails was Phillies outfielder Lenny Dykstra, all favorites because of their hard-nosed play.

A linebacker and center, Bednarik was one of the last great two-way players in NFL history. His brain-jarring hit on New York Giants running back Frank Gifford in a 1960 game still reverberates in NFL lore.

In the 1970s, Schultz earned his reputation as an enforcer, ready to drop his gloves on a moment's notice. With his rugged play, Schultz helped the "Broad Street Bullies" to two Stanley Cups. In 1974–75, Schultz compiled a record 472 penalty minutes.

Before he was sent to prison for bankruptcy fraud, Dykstra, a former all-star center fielder, was held in high regard for his gutsy style of play with the New York Mets and Phillies.

"Concrete Charlie, Hammer, and Nails, this isn't so much a sports town as a hardware store," quipped one sports writer.

TRAIN WRECK

Muhammad Ali was a big draw wherever he fought. One particular time he was in Inglewood, California, and hotel rooms were scarce, as one British journalist found. The journalist was forced to take a room out of town the day before the fight.

Unfortunately, his hotel was located near a train station. Hour after hour a train would pull in and come to a screeching halt. Needless to say, the writer was unable to get any sound sleep.

Finally, the frustrated journalist called the front desk and issued this memorable line:

"I say, old chap, can you tell me what time my room gets into Inglewood?"

CALLING IT LIKE HE SEES IT

As the longtime broadcaster for the Los Angeles Dodgers, Vin Scully has called just about everything imaginable in baseball, from perfect games to pennant winners. Only one thing eluded him in more than 50 years in the Dodgers broadcast booth—until the 2007 season, that is:

Say three words: WHO'S ON FIRST?

The famous skit by old-time comic duo Abbott and Costello is an American classic. And finally, Scully got to weave the famous line into a Dodgers broadcast.

Chin-Lung Hu, a native of Taiwan, was a September call-up in 2007. Hu, pronounced *who*, homered in his first hit as a Dodger in a game with the San Diego Padres.

In his second game, Hu went 0-for-4.

Now it was Hu's third game. The Dodgers were playing the Arizona Diamondbacks, and Scully was still waiting for him to visit first base.

"Let's hope Hu gets a base hit, folks. I can't wait to say, *who*'s on first," Scully said.

The third time was the charm for Scully as Hu whacked a single. The announcer got help from his audience.

"Okay, everybody," Scully said. "All together . . . WHO's on first?"

Abbott and Costello had to be smiling down from Comic Heaven.

HAPLESS HITTER

Despite pitching 15 years in the major leagues, including an appearance in the World Series, those accomplishments weren't highlighted in Bob Buhl's obituary in the *New York Times* in 2001.

The focus of the obit was a negative record he set during the 1962 season. That year, he went hitless in 70 at-bats, striking out 36 times.

"I was probably the worst hitter in baseball," Buhl once said in an interview. "I can't remember any pitcher I could hit."

The headline of the obit was unkind, but told the story succinctly:

"Bob Buhl, 72, Braves Pitcher Hapless as a Hitter."

GETTING HIS PRIORITIES STRAIGHT

On more than one occasion since retiring from elite competition in 1985, downhill skiing star Franz Klammer won a Jeep for finishing first in a legends ski event. Each time, he gave the vehicle away.

"I race for the glory of being fast, not for a prize," Klammer said, ". . . unless the prize is a Mercedes.

SERVES HIM RIGHT

Roger Goodell, Public Enemy Number One in New Orleans.

At least that's how Louisianans felt about the NFL commissioner after his crackdown following the bounty scandal in 2012. Goodell came down hard on the Saints—some thought too hard—and handed out several suspensions, including one for a year to head coach Sean Payton.

Saints fans felt the suspensions cost the team a chance to play in the Super Bowl on their own field. And they showed their displeasure. As the city geared up to host Super Bowl XLVII without the Saints, there were signs in restaurants all over town with the Commissioner's photo and caption,

"Don't Serve This Man" and "Don't Feed the Commissioner."

Leading up to the game, they had debated on sports talk radio shows how to treat the visiting commissioner.

Two typical reactions:

At Zeus' Place, a pet boarding and grooming business, photos of Goodell lined boxes of kitty litter. And Kathy Anderson, owner of the Parkview Tavern in Mid-City, had a photo of Goodell taped over its dartboard since the start of the season.

"[Goodell] represents our season that could've been, should've been, and wasn't," Anderson said.

ODDBALLS

The San Francisco Giants were visiting the White House following their victory over the Texas Rangers in the 2010 World Series. President Barack Obama greeted the Giants, acknowledging they were a rather oddball bunch.

Obama referred to the Giants as "baseball's characters with character."

Obama especially singled out quirky relief ace Brian Wilson, famed for his foot-long beard, tattoos, and Mohawk hairstyle, and Tim Lincecum, known as the "The Freak" for his ability to throw fastballs despite a relatively small frame.

"The Giants may be a little different," the president said, "but one thing they know is how to win."

CHICKEN-ING OUT

For Wade Boggs, it was all about the preparation.

While winning batting championships for the Boston Red Sox, the Hall of Fame third baseman religiously followed a routine before games. When the Red Sox were home, Boggs ate chicken every day with wife Debbie and daughter Meagan.

"My stomach always required mild foods, so I was eating chicken three or four times a week in 1977 when I was playing in Winston-Salem," he said. "I noticed that I always seemed to hit best after chicken. So I started having Debbie fix it every day."

Boggs's favorite was his wife's lemon chicken, which he ate once a week.

Following a precise routine, Boggs then left his apartment for Fenway Park at 3:00 o'clock every game day. Simple explanation: "That way it's almost always between 3:10 and 3:15 when I walk in the door of the clubhouse."

Why not? It worked for Boggs, who was a five-time AL batting champion with a .328 lifetime average

THE DAY THEY BOOED SANTA

They call Philadelphia the "City of Brotherly Love." Except when it comes to sports, of course.

Philadelphia sports fans have developed a well-deserved reputation for sick behavior: pelting rival players and coaches with batteries; cheering when an opposing player is seriously injured; and forcing a Phillies forfeit because of a bottle-tossing incident.

Philadelphia fans are particularly known for their capacity to boo. But boo Santa Claus?

It happened on December 15, 1968.

Winding down a terrible season, the Eagles were hosting the Minnesota Vikings.

It was time for the halftime show. The 19-year-old Frank Olivo was summoned from the stands to stand in for the usual Santa, a hired pro who was stranded in a snowstorm.

Olivo, who had taken to wearing a Christmas outfit at Eagles games, rushed into action. He whipped on the Santa suit, then made his entrance onto the field through a human corridor of cheerleaders dressed as elves. A band struck up "Here Comes Santa Claus."

As Olivo jogged across the field, he was greeted by a chorus of boos.

"Boos rolled like thunder from the stands," noted one sports writer.

It was nothing compared to the hostile reception he got next: A hail of icy, tightly packed snowballs came flying out at Olivo. He answered the target practice by raising a stiff middle finger at the fans, which also included children.

A Philadelphia sports radio host was disgusted by the display of human indignity. He likened it to "spitting on Miss America."

Several years later, Olivo was asked to dress up in the same Santa suit for a 76ers game, and guess what happened?

History repeats.

SPORTS HOOLIGANS

When Veterans Stadium was operational in Philadelphia, it was regarded as one of the rowdiest ballparks in America.

Hooligan behavior at the old ballpark was greeted with unusual measures.

How unusual? On football game day, a courthouse was installed in the bowels of the stadium. There was a judge and jail to deal with criminal behavior.

After watching the football players slam each other, the rowdy participants were on their way to the slammer.

GLASSY STARE

During the 1990s, Eagles owner Norman Braman was going through agony in his luxury box watching his inept team on the way to another loss.

He was frustrated, but no more so than Philadelphia mayor Ed Rendell, a passionate Eagles fan sitting in the box just next door.

From time to time, Rendell would bang on the glass separating his box from the Eagles owner and shout, "Norman, do something!"

Braman did—he had blinds installed over the glass.

GIVE HIM A HAND

The merciless Philadelphia sports fans sank to a new low in the case of Mathew Scott.

Scott was one of the first recipients of a hand transplant in America. In recognition of his historic surgery, Scott was invited to throw out the ceremonial first pitch at a Phillies game opening the season.

Scott's toss bounced across the plate.

The crowd booed. It wasn't what he expected.

Noted Angelo Cataldi, host of a local sports talk show:

"The guy's looking around like, 'Oh, good, I just got out of a hospital bed. I've still got the sutures here. I get booed because I didn't throw a strike.'"

TALK ABOUT TOUGH FANS

Football coach Andy Reid got a taste of the Philadelphia sports fans' attitude when he was once introduced at a Flyers hockey game.

As Reid stood up to acknowledge his recognition, he was booed lustily by the crowd. It didn't seem to matter to fans that he had yet to coach a game for the Eagles. As it turned out, Reid remained for 14 seasons, plenty of time for the fans to express their opinions.

THE UNKNOWN BASEBALL PLAYER

Few baseball players had a love-hate relationship like Mike Schmidt did with Phillies fans.

Although Schmidt hit 548 home runs, won three MVP awards, and led the Phillies to a World Series title in 1980, the Hall of Fame third baseman was not a fan favorite in Philly for reasons not explainable.

Except rarely, when he stepped onto the field wearing a disguise.

The Phillies were taking infield practice one day when the familiar number 20 walked onto the field wearing a blond wig and sunglasses. Schmidt had decided to have some fun with the fans.

For a change, Schmidt heard laughter and applause instead of boos.

TYING ONE ON

The history of brawling among fans at Flyers hockey games has been well documented. But fans brawling with the other team's players?

Yes, it actually happened during a Flyers game with the Toronto Maple Leafs in 2001.

Toronto's Tie Domi was in the penalty box when a drunken Flyers fan broke the glass and attacked the Maple Leaf player. He soon regretted his action.

Domi turned on his attacker, giving him a sound thrashing.

Suffice it to say Domi was not penalized for fighting.

10

CAN YOU BELIEVE IT?

If Diego Maradona's 1986 World Cup score against England is considered the "Hand of God" goal, the folks in Ireland see Thierry Henry's role in France's draw with their national team in 2009 that kept Ireland out of the World Cup as the "Hand of the Godless" goal.

To Soviet citizens and athletes in 1972, their basketball team's victory over the United States for Olympic gold was fair and faultless. To Americans, it remains a travesty, and their team's silver medals remain unclaimed.

Botched calls generally are a matter of perspective. And for nearly every incorrect, improper, or uninformed decision, there is someone who also profited from it.

Which not only makes for great sports arguments, but for another chapter in the world of Crazyball.

BASEBALL

Imperfect Call

No matter what Jim Joyce does the rest of his career, he will be remembered for robbing Armando Galarraga of a perfect game.

Not a bad thing at all for an opponent getting a solid hit to end a no-hitter. But hardly the kind of epitaph any umpire wants.

Yet it's all Joyce's, thanks to his decision on June 2, 2010, that has gone down as one of the most egregious blown calls in baseball annals.

That Joyce made the mistake was stunning in itself. He was a seasoned ump who weeks earlier had worked second base during another perfect game, by Oakland's Dallas Braden. The pressure of tough calls in tight situations usually brought out the best in Joyce.

Galarraga got the first out of the ninth on a fly ball. The second came on a groundout, with Joyce making the correct call at first base.

The final out in Galarraga's gem would be Jason Donald, and he obliged with a grounder to the right side, where first baseman Miguel Cabrera ranged over, grabbed it, and threw to Galarraga covering the bag.

"Something just instinctually, instinctively, told me he was safe," Joyce said.

He wasn't, as replays immediately showed. The fans at Tiger Stadium and most of the Tigers protested loudly, and soon Joyce realized he'd made the ultimate error to take away the ultimate pitching achievement from Galarraga.

"I have replayed that play so many times, my head hurts,"Joyce said days later. "All I can see is Armando Galarraga's face. He didn't say a word to me. I can see his face and him not saying anything. When that happens, you think you're right."

Galarraga took the gaffe better than just about anyone else, retiring the next batter for his "one-hitter." By the time Joyce reached the umpires' room beneath the stands, he was telling his fellow umps, "I hope I got it right."

Upon confirming that he blew it by watching the replay, Joyce was astonished how obvious it was that Donald was out. And he was enraged at himself.

The next day, Commissioner Bud Selig said he could not reverse the decision and award Galarraga a perfecto. That didn't cheer up Joyce.

"I didn't want this to be my 15 minutes of fame," he said. "I would have liked my 15 minutes to be a great call in the World Series. Hopefully, my 15 minutes are over now."

Not quite: Joyce and Galarraga combined to write a book about the call, and Joyce was banned from ever again working a game involving Galarraga's team.

Thanks, Kid

Orioles-Yankees, already a high-pitched American League rivalry in 1996, reached a fevered pitch in 1996.

Baltimore led Game 1 of the AL championship series 4-3 in the eighth inning, with AL rookie of the year Derek Jeter at bat. Not quite a power hitter, the shortstop lifted a fly ball into right field that was deep enough to be threatening, but seemed likely to hit off the wall. Maybe a double for Jeter.

As right fielder Tony Tarasco drifted back toward the stands, he bumped the wall, probably damaging any chance of catching the ball.

But someone else had a bead on Jeter's hit: a 12-year-old from New Jersey named Jeffrey Maier.

Maier stuck his black baseball glove beyond the first row of seats, over the wall, and pulled the ball into the stands, although he didn't catch it. As Tarasco gestured for fan interference, the only one who really counted in determining the outcome, umpire Rich Garcia, instead signaled home run.

A lengthy argument ensued, but with no video replay allowed for umpires at the time, the call stood, even though replays distinctly showed Maier interfering. In fact, Garcia admitted after the game that the ball would not have gone over the fence without Maier's assistance.

Three innings later, Bernie Williams homered for the Yankees to win 5-4. They won the series four games to one and then took the World Series over Atlanta.

Moments after the game ended, the Orioles filed a protest with commissioner Bud Selig, declaring that "the best interests of baseball demand that this wrong be righted."

Selig did not concur, further inciting the folks in Baltimore, as well as media that dug their tongues deep into their cheeks and offered advice on how to get revenge.

Such as this from *Baltimore Sun* columnist Ken Rosenthal:

"Drop your wine and cheese and get dirty. If your seats are in the front row in left field make like young Jeff and bring your fish nets and oversized gloves. Better yet, donate your ticket to the nearest 7-footer you can find, and the first time the Orioles hit a long fly to left, watch him put Tim Raines in a headlock. You want interference? Baltimore can do interference."

Maier, meanwhile, became a hero to all Yankees fans, and especially to his classmates and fellow townies in Old Tappan, a suburban community northwest of the Bronx.

"It's a one-in-a-million chance to do that kind of stuff. You wish it could happen to you," said 14-year-old Daniel Lysogorsky.

And the Old Tappan Deli, which delivered lunch daily to Maier's school, offered The Jeff Maier Special of turkey sandwich, cherry Coke, and small pretzels for $4.75.

But Hall of Famer Reggie Jackson wasn't so impressed by Maier's glove work:

"If the kid keeps playing like he did last night, he's going to be a DH, I can tell you that."

Phantom Tag

Fenway Park. Ninth inning of a tight playoff game between mega-rivals. A potential rally for the Boston Red Sox against the New York Yankees—what could be better in Beantown?

The venerable stadium was rocking as the Red Sox, trailing 3-2 in the eighth inning, had Jose Offerman on first base. John Valentin's ground ball seemed too slow for a double play, and Yankees second baseman Chuck Knoblauch made a cursory attempt at a tag on Offerman before throwing to first.

Knoblauch missed Offerman by a few feet. Everyone in Fenway saw it—except umpire Tim Tschida. He called Offerman out, and the Yankees got a double play.

Red Sox manager Jimy Williams stormed onto the field to protest, to no avail.

Worse yet for New Englanders, the Yankees scored six times in the ninth and won going away. Williams also was ejected for throwing his cap after arguing another call. Fenway fans, still enraged, released their anger by throwing anything they could find onto the field during that inning.

Play was halted, with police and stadium security taking the field to settle down the crowd before the teams could resume. Players from the Yankees' bullpen headed to the safety of the dugout during the fan protests.

"ROBBED AGAIN," was the headline the next day in the *Boston Herald*, accompanied by a photo clearly showing it was a phantom tag by Knoblauch.

The Yankees closed out the series in their next meeting. And to twist the dagger into Bostonians, the Yanks also won the World Series.

Wait, it gets even worse for the Sox and their followers: Tschida later admitted he blew the call.

"I didn't make the right call," Tschida said. "It's a very difficult play to get in the position you want. And that's a frustrating thing for an umpire, because we like to call everything properly.

"It appeared to me as though he got him."

Got him? Didn't even come close enough to hug him.

Pine Tar

Mention the words "pine tar," and one name in baseball instantly comes to mind: George Brett.

For years, players used pine tar on the bats to help with the grip. The New York Yankees believed Brett, the future Hall of Fame third baseman of the Kansas City Royals, rubbed the stuff onto his Louisville slugger a bit too much, and that it was an advantage in a 1983 game in the Bronx.

With two outs and a runner on base in the ninth inning, the Yankees led 4-3. Their closer, the menacing Goose Gossage—himself later a Hall of Fame inductee—was chucking fastballs to Brett, looking to save the win. Instead, Brett laced into one and sent it deep into the right field stands, giving KC the lead.

After Brett's slow circuit of the bases, out of the Yankees' dugout bolted manager Billy Martin. He pointed to Brett's bat, and insisted that home plate umpire Tim McClelland examine it for too much pine tar.

Martin noted the rule prohibiting more than 18 inches of pine tar on a bat, claiming Brett had exceeded it.

Brett was seated in the Royals' dugout, a confused but not worried look on his face about the commotion at home plate. Dutifully, McClelland walked over toward the Royals' dugout, grabbed the bat, and decided to measure it at home plate, which is 17 inches wide.

Sure enough, he discovered there was too much pine tar.

What next? Even the umpiring crew was unsure, so McClelland looked at the rule book before dramatically walking toward where Brett was seated, the bat still in the ump's right hand. He looked at Brett and signaled him out.

No home run. Illegal bat. Batter out, game over, Yankees win.

An enraged Brett sprinted from his seat and up the dugout steps and confronted all four umpires, gesturing, screaming, acting like a man who had been, well, robbed in broad daylight. The smirk on Martin's face didn't help matters, either.

Had Brett gotten the opportunity, he might have hauled off and slugged McClelland, he was so incensed.

"The sight of George coming out of the dugout is etched in my mind forever," Yankees first baseman Don Mattingly told ESPN.com years later. "That roar symbolizes the way he plays the game, the kind of fire he has."

This was one fire out of control.

Brett and the Royals made sure the story would not end there.

Naturally, they filed a protest with American League president Lee McPhail. It took McPhail four days to rule, and shockingly, he didn't uphold McClelland's decision. Instead, he determined that the bat should have been removed from the game, and that the game be resumed at a later date—with the Royals in front 5-4 and the homer counting.

None too pleased, McClelland insisted, "We can't arbitrarily rule on which rules we're going to enforce." And the Yankees found any way they could think of, including going to court, to block the resumption of the contest.

But they eventually were overruled, only to stage more shenanigans when the replay began—without Brett, who, remember, had been ejected for his tirade that had become a worthwhile endeavor for the star third baseman.

Martin first protested that Brett missed first base, then second base. The new umpiring crew signaled safe, and was protected by a letter from the original umpires saying all bases had been touched on Brett's shot.

Ace reliever Dan Quisenberry retired the Yankees in order in the bottom of the ninth, and the Pine Tar Game ended 25 days after it began.

Martin's smirk long since had disappeared.

All It Cost Was a World Series

Look at the record books and under 1985, it says World Series winners: Kansas City Royals.

That was the end result of probably the biggest blown call in baseball championship annals.

St. Louis led the Series with Interstate 70 rival Kansas City three games to two, and was up 1-0 in the sixth game when the Royals came to bat in the bottom of the ninth. Outstanding reliever Todd Worrell, virtually untouchable all season, was on the mound, hoping to clinch the team's second title in four seasons.

He immediately induced pinch hitter Jorge Orta to hit a chopper to the right side, a routine play. First baseman Jack Clark fielded the ball and flipped it to Worrell, covering the bag, seemingly in plenty of time.

Don Deckinger didn't think so and signaled safe. Video replays clearly showed Orta was, uh, Outa.

"If that doesn't happen, we probably don't win," said the Royals' Hal McRae.

Cardinals manager Whitey Herzog argued vehemently and Worrell even reenacted his performance on the play. Replays on the stadium scoreboard made it even more obvious that Deckinger missed the call, but umpires couldn't consult them.

And the game went on. Because this was simply the first hitter of the inning, and Worrell was almost an impregnable force, St. Louis still appeared to be in good shape.

Except the Cardinals fell apart, perhaps unnerved by Deckinger's gaffe. An error, a passed ball, a few hits—including Dane Iorg's game-winner—and KC had a 2-1 victory.

Stripped clean of their emotions and, well, their confidence, the Cardinals fell 11-0 in Game 7 as the Royals won their only World Series crown.

Deckinger, who never apologized for the decision—he even kept his same phone number, which led to a flood of nasty phone calls—spoke with MLB commissioner Peter Ueberroth after the game.

"I immediately asked him if I got it right or wrong, because up to that point I didn't know," Deckinger told ESPN.com. "He said, 'No, I don't think so. I don't think you got it right.' You just get that sick feeling."

Eventually, though, he accepted what history has determined to be an awful error, and Deckinger even owned a painting of the play in later years.

Angel, What Have You Done?

Nicknamed "Blue" because of the outfits they wear, umpires will argue until they are blue in the face that one botched call doesn't lead to another.

Evidence in 2013 proved the opposite, and it led to suspensions, bad press for the arbiters of the game, and a demand for more use of instant replay to help the umpires.

Most egregious were two decisions, one missing a home run and the other misinterpreting the rules. It doesn't get more Crazyball than that for umps.

Oakland's Adam Rosales sent a ninth-inning shot to left field that went over the 19-foot-high outfield wall in Cleveland, striking a metal railing. It should have been called a game-tying home run, but instead was ruled a double. As Rosales stood on second base, A's manager Bob Melvin challenged the call and, as was his right, asked for a video review.

Off trudged three of the four umps to the replay area set up for them. They took their time, returned to the field—and blew it. Rosales was ordered to stay at second, despite indisputable video evidence he'd hit the ball out of the park.

The next day, MLB executive vice president Joe Torre said an "improper call" was made. In other words, WRONG!!!!

It helped cost Oakland the game, because the A's couldn't bring Rosales around to score and lost 4-3. Even worse, they lost the next day 9-2 to be swept by Cleveland, only to find out they'd been fleeced the previous night.

"By rule, the decision to reverse a call by use of instant replay is at the sole discretion of the crew chief," Torre said. "In the opinion of Angel Hernandez . . . there was not clear and convincing evidence to overturn the decision on the field. It was a judgment call, and as such, it stands as final.

"Home and away broadcast feeds are available for all uses of instant replay, and they were available to the crew. . . . Given what we saw, we recognize that an improper call was made. Perfection is an impossible standard in any endeavor, but our goal is always to get the calls right."

Yet on the very day Torre made his comments, another umpiring crew messed up, this time in Houston.

In the seventh inning, with two outs and the Astros ahead 5-3, Houston brought in reliever Wesley Wright. He threw some warm-up pitches from the mound before manager Bo Porter sprinted from the dugout to stop Wright. Porter brought in another reliever, Hector Ambriz.

Angels manager Mike Scioscia then confronted the umpires, saying, correctly, that Wright couldn't leave without pitching to at least one batter. Yet the umpires let Ambriz stay in, and Scioscia filed a protest.

His protest didn't matter, because the Angels came back and won 6-5. But the umpires' error would not go unnoticed or unpunished by MLB.

Fieldin Culbreth was suspended for two games because he was the crew chief. Culbreth and the rest of his crew—Brian O'Nora, Bill Welke, and Adrian Johnson—were also fined.

"We just got to cross-sectioning different rules within the changing of a pitcher, and just had a hard time getting back on track from that," Culbreth said. "We got confused."

Not a very comforting thought.

BASKETBALL

Give Them Another Try—And Another

The United States had never lost in Olympic basketball. Not one game, let alone a gold medal contest.

That stream of success was built with college players and other amateurs. Nobody from the NBA was allowed to play before 1992.

By the 1972 Munich Games, many countries, particularly the Soviet Union, had national squads, men who were paid solely to play hoops. These were adults playing against college kids, and while U.S. basketball still was at the pinnacle of the sport, the gap with international play had narrowed.

Indeed, the Soviets had played some 400 games together. The U.S. collegians had 12 as a unit before reaching Germany.

With the help of the most outrageous officiating imaginable, including interference from the head of the international basketball federation, the Americans saw their streak snapped by the Soviets.

The USSR had a formidable team and was a worthy challenger to the United States. Plus, under coach Hank Iba, the Americans played a slowdown style that played directly into the hands of the physical, sometimes brutish Soviets. With a more up-tempo pace under a different coach, the Americans might have run away from the Soviets.

"They knew what they were getting when they picked Coach Iba," USC guard Paul Westphal said. "They weren't picking a guy who's going to go out there and press and run and play basketball the way American basketball was being played at that time."

Instead, the gold medal match was a struggle in which the U.S. trailed by as many as 10 points while seeking its 64th straight Olympic victory.

Then the Americans rallied, and Doug Collins stole a pass and was fouled with 10 seconds left. The Americans trailed by one point.

Calmly, Collins sank both free throws for a 50-49 lead—the first of the game for the US.

Then things got crazyball.

The Soviets in-bounded, but the referees blew their whistles to halt play, discussing whether the USSR coach had called a timeout. Once determined they hadn't, a second in-bounds play came, the Soviets couldn't convert, and the Americans exulted, gold medals almost in hand.

But the scorer's table had not reset the clock to show three seconds. That's where William Jones, the secretary general of FIBA, the international governing body for basketball, stepped in. Jones insisted the second play couldn't count because the clock was not reset. He ordered a third replay, with :03 showing on the scoreboard.

Jones was often described as a "friend" of the Soviets, and to this day the Americans will cite that comfortable arrangement as a factor in the mayhem and the end of the game.

The Soviets were given yet another opportunity to try a long in-bounds pass.

"We couldn't believe that they were giving them all these chances," U.S. forward Mike Bantom said. "It was like they were going to let them do it until they got it right."

Well, they got it right on the third try. Alexander Belov jumped high between two American defenders, using some physical force to get the ball, then made the winning layup as the buzzer once again sounded.

This time, the game was officially over, with the USSR winning 52-51.

Immediately, the U.S. team filed a protest, but with Jones involved in the final decision and a five-member panel that included three pro-Soviet nations hearing the appeal, the Americans were cooked.

As a final act of protest, the Americans refused their silver medals, leaving the medal stand empty during the awards ceremony.

"We didn't earn the silver," team captain Kenny Davis often has said. "We earned the gold. All these years later, not one player on our team has come forward to accept the silver medal."

And almost certainly they never will.

BOXING

Stolen In Seoul

Sometimes a decision is so inaccurate, so dubious, that it renders more than outrage. It leads to changes in a sport.

Roy Jones Jr's loss by decision to Park Si-hun of the host country at the 1988 Seoul Olympics remains amateur boxing's biggest blemish, as glaring as any cut, welt, or black eye anyone has received in the ring. And the apparent reasoning behind it is as bogus as Park's victory.

Considered the best gold medal hope on the U.S. team, Jones so manhandled Park that he landed 86 punches to the South Korean's 32. Twice, Park took standing-8 counts, and he was in trouble for most of the three rounds against his faster, stronger opponent.

Then came the judges' ruling: Park won a majority decision.

How? Legend has it that several of the five judges didn't want Park embarrassed by losing a 5-0 decision in front of the home crowd, even though the fans were prepared for just that. So they voted for Park, believing each of the other four would give Jones his well-earned win.

Park even apologized to Jones afterward, and one judge eventually acknowledged his decision was a mistake.

Four years later, computerized scoring had come to the Olympics—although bad calls since became common. It was some small progress, at least, although they were planning to use pro style judging at the 2016 Rio Games.

Not that the decision hurt Jones: He went on to one of the most successful and lucrative professional careers in boxing history.

FOOTBALL

He Called What?

Perhaps the easiest call in all of football is on the coin toss. So how did Abner Haynes and Jerome Bettis get it so wrong?

Let us count the ways.

Haynes's faux pas could have been severe because it came in the AFL championship game in 1962. Bettis's bobble, if it actually was that, occurred in a 1998 Thanksgiving Day game between Pittsburgh and Detroit.

Haynes was the star running back of the Dallas Texans, who, unbeknown to most everyone, were playing their final game before moving to Kansas City and becoming the Chiefs. The title contest against the Oilers had gone to overtime in windy Houston.

As the visiting captain, Haynes went out for the OT coin toss, told by coach Hank Stram that the Texans wanted the wind at their backs.

"If we win the toss, we don't want to receive," Stram told Haynes. "If they win the toss, we want to kick to the clock."

Somewhere between the sideline and midfield, Haynes got confused. He sure enough won the toss and told the referee: "We'll kick to the clock."

Once Haynes said the Texans would kick, it didn't matter what else he mentioned. He should have said they would defend the goal that gave them the wind at their backs.

Houston's Al Jamison immediately took the end Stram wanted, and he was celebrating exuberantly as he headed back to the huddle.

Haynes was stunned as he went back to Stram.

"How did they get the ball and get the wind?" he asked Haynes, who couldn't fathom he had messed up something so easy.

"I just accepted it. You can't do it over," Stram admitted. "I didn't say much. It was over. You just forget about it and go out and try to win the game."

Which Dallas did, in the second OT on a wind-aided 25-yard field goal by Tommy Brooker—after the teams had switched sides.

Bettis's Steelers weren't so fortunate.

The outstanding running back claimed he called tails for the OT toss, but referee Phil Luckett said he heard "heads/tails" and went with the first word he heard. When it came up tails, Luckett gave the Lions the option and, naturally, they took the ball—while Bettis screamed bloody murder, to no avail.

Detroit won, and the league soon changed the procedure so that the call was made before the ref tossed the coin, and the ref would repeat what was called.

Didn't help the Steelers much on a Thanksgiving Day when they had little to be thankful for.

No Video Allowed

The use of video replays to help NFL officials had died an ugly death in 1992 because of its inconsistencies and how much coaches disliked it. It took another six years, and a blown call that cost a team a game and possible a playoff berth, for it to reappear. And remain.

Seattle led the New York Jets 31-26 in the final moments at Giants Stadium, but the Jets were threatening. They got down to the Seahawks' 5-yard line and, with 20 seconds left, on fourth down, Vinny Testaverde scrambled down the middle and dived for the end zone.

The quarterback's helmet got over the goal line. The ball, as replays clearly showed, did not. Yet the call was a TD.

But because game officials no longer could use video reviews, the "Phantom Touchdown" stood. New York won, 32-31, eventually moving on to the AFC title game.

After being whistled for unsportsmanlike conduct for throwing his helmet following the touchdown, Seahawks cornerback Shawn Springs wondered if the officials had been "intimidated."

"The refs should really let the players decide the game," Springs said. "Don't make a call that determines the outcome."

Even worse, Seattle finished 8-8 that season, just missing the playoffs, and coach Dennis Erickson wound up getting fired.

At the next league meetings, owners voted replay reviews back in as an officiating aid.

Let's Go to the Videotape—and Still Get It Wrong

Fourteen years after his helmet scored a touchdown, Testaverde had to laugh when game officials completely blew another call—and it also had major ramifications.

Green Bay led its Week 3 Monday night game at Seattle 12-7 when the Seahawks reached the Packers' 24-yard line for the final play. QB Russell Wilson chucked a prayer into the end zone, where his receiver, Golden Tate, clearly shoved cornerback Sam Shields to the ground.

No flag from the replacement officials—the regulars had been locked out by the league since before the preseason began.

Tate and defensive back M. D. Jennings leaped for possession, with Jennings seemingly in control, only to have one official signal dead ball and the other signal touchdown. Total confusion.

Somehow, the ruling was touchdown, with Tate reasoning, "I don't even know the rule but I guess the tie goes to the receiver."

Even if there was no tie until Tate wrestled Jennings for the ball when they both reached the ground?

Referee Wayne Elliott, in what would be his final act in the NFL, went under the hood—and still blew it, confirming a TD. Ten minutes after the controversial final play, the Seahawks kicked a meaningless extra point to win 14-12.

As The Associated Press reported: "Replacement ref rage may have peaked Monday night."

"Don't ask me a question about the officials," Green Bay coach Mike McCarthy said. "I've never seen anything like that in all my years in football."

Nor did the NFL ever want to see anything like it again.

Two days later, the league had settled with the regular officials, who were back on the field—to warm welcomes from the players, coaches, and, yes, even fans—for a Thursday-night game in Baltimore.

Fifth Down and One

The Missouri Tigers know how to count to five downs. That didn't help them in 1990.

Colorado was the beneficiary of the officials' inability to figure out what down it was, and the Buffaloes wound up winning the national championship later that season.

When the Buffs, ranked 12th in the nation, visited Missouri, they trailed 31-27 with 2:25 remaining and had the ball at their 12. They quickly moved downfield, getting to the Mizzou 3 with 31 seconds to go.

Plenty of time and, it would turn out, more than enough opportunities to score.

After a spike, star running back Eric Bieniemy was stuffed just before reaching the goal line. Third-and-goal from the 1.

But the official—actually, a volunteer—on the sideline had not moved the down marker to 3. Referee J.C. Louderback and his staff didn't notice.

Bieniemy went nowhere on what should have been a third-down run. As the marker was moved to 3 when it really was fourth down, QB Charles Johnson spiked the ball, believing the Buffs had another down coming.

Even though they didn't, they were given it. Missouri fans screamed from the stands that it was fifth down, and the media in the press box knew it, as well. Yet no one on the field figured it out.

Johnson then ran into a pile and was judged to have squeezed into the end zone—even as Missouri fans stormed onto the field thinking the Tigers had triumphed. Their celebrations soon turned into angry protestations over a 33-31 defeat.

"I'm not hiding anything," Louderback told Rivals.com. "I've always said when there's an error, you stand up and say exactly what happened and you don't hide from it.

"I've got a poker group that brings it up every night we play. We'd go every other week and someone's always bringing up, 'How's our fifth-down man?'"

He's not the only fifth-down ref, but at least another incident had a fairer ending.

Fifty years before the unfortunate Miscount in Mizzou, there was the famous Cornell-Dartmouth "Fifth Down" game.

Cornell had gone ahead of Dartmouth 7-3 with a late touchdown that apparently gave the Big Red the victory.

Not so fast.

Referee William "Red" Friesell submitted a report admitting he had made a mistake in allowing Cornell an extra down, on which they scored.

Dartmouth coach Red Blaik, who would go on to everlasting fame as Army's head coach, had watched as Cornell turned the extra down into a touchdown from the Big Red 6-yard line. On what was really fifth down, Walter Scholl passed to Bill Murphy for the go-ahead TD.

It didn't hold up after referee Friesell submitted his report.

Cornell athletic director James Lynah and football coach Carl Snavely informed Dartmouth:

"In view of the conclusions reached by the officials that the Cornell touchdown was scored on a fifth down, Cornell relinquishes claim to the victory and extends congratulations to Dartmouth."

Giving up the victory was quite a sacrifice for the Big Red, who were on an 18-game winning streak and ranked No. 2 in the nation.

Blaik publicly remained silent while media reported the extra down and Eastern Intercollegiate Football Association officials investigated. Privately, he stewed about being robbed.

Then Cornell did the honorable thing.

But Friesell didn't escape unscathed. He often was ridiculed by fans the rest of that season, with one sending him an abacus in the mail, suggesting he use it in an upcoming game.

HOCKEY

Hull of a Blown Call

Having seen too much net-crashing and abuse of goalies, the NHL had gotten very diligent about protecting the netminders. It passed a rule disallowing any goals if a player from the attacking team was in the crease before the puck.

The league was so serious about it that video replays were used to determine whether goals should count. But the rule was so black-and-white in nature that even when a player had the tip of his skate inside the goalie's area, yet was not directly involved in the play or the shot on net, the score would be negated.

Controversy followed the rule everywhere, and in Game 6 of the 1999 Stanley Cup finals, with Dallas a victory away from skating off with the trophy, the rule blew up on the NHL.

The game headed into overtime tied 1-1. Then into a second extra period and, finally, exhaustingly, into a third.

Brett Hull, one of hockey's most dangerous scorers and a future Hall of Famer, got open in front of Sabres goalie Dominik Hasek. His shot was stopped by Hasek, and then the fun (for Dallas fans) and horror (for Buffalo fans) began.

Hull entered the crease while kicking the puck from his skate to his stick. His foot clearly was inside the blue paint of the goaltender's territory even though the puck had gone outside the area, then back in. With his left skate firmly inside the crease, Hull shot—and scored the Cup-winning goal.

Throughout the 1998–99 season and for much of the playoffs, such a goal would have been waved off. Not this time, and as the Stars' wild celebrations began, the Sabres protested to no avail.

The league's explanation, as described by supervisor of officials Bryan Lewis:

"A puck that rebounds off the goalie, the goal post, or an opposing player is not deemed to be a change of possession, and therefore Hull would be deemed to be in possession or control of the puck, allowed to shoot and score a goal even though the one foot would be in the crease in advance of the puck.

"Hull had possession and control of the puck. The rebound off the goalie does not change anything. It is his puck then to shoot and score, albeit a foot may or may not be in the crease prior to."

In other words, even though Hull was attached in no way to the puck at one key juncture, even with his skate in the crease, he still was judged to be in possession?

Almost sounds like the NHL was making up rules as it went along.

"We all knew that they had changed the rule," Hull said years later. "But obviously the NHL decided they weren't going to tell anybody but the teams . . . They changed the rule to say if you have control in the crease, you can score the goal, and that's exactly what it was.

"But nobody knows that. You can tell people that a million times and they just will not listen."

Especially if they are Sabres fans.

Pull the Goalie?

Often lost in the mayhem of the "Miracle on Ice" is the fact that Soviet coach Viktor Tikhonov made two wrong decisions regarding his goalies in the 1980 classic against the Americans.

Tikhonov was fortunate through much of his career behind the Soviet Union's bench that Vladislav Tretiak was his netminder. From the legendary 1972 Summit Series between the USSR and Canada through a slew of Olympics, Tretiak was the man in the net, and the Soviets usually were skating off with gold.

At Lake Placid, in their medals-round matchup with the United States, Tretiak was where he belonged. But not for long.

At the very end of the first period, Mark Johnson scored on a sloppy rebound for the Americans, tying the game 2-2. Shockingly, Tikhonov sent out backup Vladimir Mishkin for the second period, trying to motivate his players.

"It was difficult for me to sit on the bench with the score 2-2," said Tretiak, who entered the Hockey Hall of Fame with three Olympic gold medals and 10 world championships for the Soviet Union. "If I played the second and third period, the game might have turned a different way."

He didn't play, and midway through the third period, U.S. captain Mike Eruzione scored on the hockey shot heard round the world for a 4-3 lead.

Then Tikhonov really lost his way. Not used to being behind late in a game, he never pulled Mishkin for an extra attacker. In fact, two of U.S. coach Herb Brooks's assistants shouted in stunned recognition: "They're not pulling him.

He [Tikhonov] doesn't know what to do and they're not pulling him."

Tikhonov stood stone-faced behind the bench as the clock ticked away. Not once did he gesture to Mishkin to come off the ice.

Tretiak told The Associated Press he never got an apology from Tikhonov for taking him out of the game—a coaching gaffe, for sure. Tikhonov wrote in his autobiography that it was the biggest mistake of his life.

With not pulling Mishkin a close second?

Hey, He Was Offside

Offside?

Clark Gillies sure was, in Game 6 of the 1980 Stanley Cup finals. Unfortunately for the Philadelphia Flyers, the man in charge of whistling down the Islanders forward for his transgression missed the call.

And they are still bitter in Philly about it.

New York led the series 3-2 and was at home on a steamy Saturday afternoon, hoping to wrap up its first Cup crown and avoid a trip back to Philadelphia for a seventh game. In the opening period, the score 1-1, Gillies passed back to linemate Butch Goring, and the puck skidded over the blue line and out of the attacking zone. Goring brought the disc back into the Flyers' zone.

Offside, Islanders.

Except the whistle didn't blow. Philadelphia's defensemen clearly relaxed for a second or so, allowing Goring to feed Duane Sutter in front for a 2-1 lead.

The Flyers were livid. As star winger Bill Barber said after the loss:

"This is the toughest since I've been with the club. I won't forget what happened today. I mean I won't forget the officiating. The Islanders were at least two feet offside on that second goal."

When Leon Stickle was shown a video replay, he shook his head.

"I was in the right position and the puck came back across," Stickle said. "I guess I blew it. Maybe I was too close to the play. Apparently the replay showed I missed it."

Stickle was one of the league's best linesmen and he worked until 1997, so this goof didn't damage his career.

But every time Stickle went to the Spectrum in Philadelphia, the locals made sure he recalled the time he swallowed the whistle.

SOCCER

Handing It to the French

Ireland was on the verge of forcing favored France to a penalty kicks shootout to determine which team would go to the 2010 World Cup in South Africa.

To understand the magnitude of an Irish advancement, consider that soccer (football in the Old Sod) is tantamount to religion in Ireland, and the World Cup is the Vatican of sports.

The Irish were ahead 1-0 after regulation at Stade de France; the French had won the first leg in Dublin 1-0. That forced extra time in the total goals series.

Deep into overtime, Florent Malouda sent a free kick to Thierry Henry to the right of goalkeeper Shay Given. Henry stopped the ball with his left hand—he could have been hailing a taxi—then compounded the foul by using his hand again to place the ball on his outstretched right foot.

Teammate William Gallas headed in the ball and France won 2-1.

“He almost caught it and walked into the net with it,” said Robbie Keane, who scored for the Irish in the 33rd minute.

But Swedish referee Martin Hansson missed both hand balls.

Henry didn’t.

“I will be honest, it was a hand ball. But I’m not the ref,” Henry said. “I played it. The ref allowed it. That’s a question you should ask him.”

The Irish still are asking.

11

MASCOTS

Walk into Citizen's Bank Park in Philadelphia and you just might be greeted by a, well, a . . . we're not really sure what he is, but he sure is popular: the Phillie Phanatic.

Kids phlock, uh, flock to his side, hoping to get a high five, a hug, or maybe even a touch of that humongous proboscis.

The Phanatic is far from the first famous sports mascot, and many will argue he isn't the most unique or the funniest or the weirdest-looking. But considering his following and the legend created around him, he tops our list.

It's a list that includes the Chicken (originally known as the San Diego Chicken); the Stanford Tree; Otto the Orange (of Syracuse University); Harvey the Hound (of the NHL's Calgary Flames); The Gorilla (of the NBA's Phoenix Suns); Milwaukee's Racing Sausages at the Brewer games; Izzy (1996 Atlanta Olympics); Iceburgh (the NHL's Pittsburgh Penguins); Youppi! (the Expos and Canadiens in Montreal); and the Banana Slug of Cal–Santa Cruz.

A dozen dynamic deliverers of comic relief, outrageous antics, and, in one case, an infamous failure.

PHILLIE PHANATIC

Born in the Galapagos Islands, according to his biography, the Phanatic is a combination of—we don't really know and we wouldn't dare venture a guess. He's 6-foot-6 and weighs 300 pounds (mostly fat), with bright green fur, white eyeballs, black pupils, purple eyelashes, and blue eyebrows.

His physical attributes, the team's website says: Overweight, clumsy feet, extra-long beak, extra-long curled-up tongue, gawking neck, and "slight" case of body odor.

He became an official greeter at Phillies games way back in 1978, sort of a baseball version of George Jessel, while also leading cheers and downing as many Philadelphia delicacies—cheesesteaks, soft pretzels, hoagies, scrapple, and Tastykakes—as he could shove down. No wonder he has a 90-inch waist.

Naturally, his favorite movie is *Rocky* and his top tune is "Take Me Out to the Ball Game."

As he cavorts on his all-terrain vehicle on the field, no opposing player or manager is safe from his shenanigans. When he heads into the crowd, it's impossible to ignore the Phanatic because he simply won't allow it. From grabbing people's food to shining a balding fan's head to pretending to make off with a sweet young thing, the Phanatic is always a major part of the show.

He even has a hot dog launcher he uses to shoot Philly Phranks into the crowd.

Originally portrayed by Dave Raymond, an intern in the Phillies' front office—Raymond's father was college football Hall of Fame coach Tubby Raymond of the University of Delaware—the Phanatic was inducted into the Mascot Hall of Fame in 2005, a shrine created by none other than Dave Raymond.

The Phanatic also has been called into the halls of justice, prompting the *Philadelphia Daily News* to dub him a "big green litigation machine." He has been sued for causing bodily harm to an elderly woman and for injuring a young woman by throwing her into a swimming pool.

Tom Burgoyne and Matt Mehler have been more recent inhabitants of the greenwear. Burgoyne has written children's books about the mascot, dubbing himself the Phanatic's "best phriend."

Burgoyne first donned the costume in 1993 and has been as responsible as anyone for turning mascots into something more than, well, mascots. They are entertainers and sometimes that also means becoming the brunt of the joke, such as when former Dodgers manager Tommy Lasorda "slam-dunked" the Phanatic to the ground. Lasorda later insisted he "hated the thing," meaning the Phanatic, not the act of throwing him down.

Burgoyne told the *Christian Science Monitor* that he searches for people who "want to be in the act" but also scurries away when someone does not. "I can sense a vibe," he told the newspaper.

He easily could have sensed a negative vibe when he first portrayed the Phanatic, lumbering in that hefty suit, saying he was "gasping for air, thinking, 'This is terrible!'" Clearly, that feeling wore off quickly, and Burgoyne soon after admitted: "I feel like I'm reliving my childhood."

THE CHICKEN

Whether he's been called the San Diego Chicken, the Famous Chicken, or just plain Chicken, Ted Giannoulas has replicated the antics of some of the great slapstick comedians of all eras.

Although some of what he has done was scripted, generally it's an ad-lib laugh fest with Giannoulas, who has been, uh, playing Chicken since 1974.

He broke in while a student at San Diego State when a local radio station sought some fool who would wear a chicken suit and do some promotional work. For $2 an hour, Giannoulas grabbed the position.

He never let go.

Luckily for him, the Padres had no objection to his performing at their games, and Giannoulas liked the idea of seeing major league baseball for free. Then, he turned it into a career.

"It's the one magic elixir that keeps me young," says Giannoulas, whose costume has been a part of a Baseball Hall of Fame exhibit.

And Giannoulas has kept them laughing with stunts such as dance-offs in which he loses, only to maul the opponent before walking off triumphant.

Or flashing an eye chart at umpires. Or doing what any good hen would, and laying an egg or two.

But he's also had his legal problems, once being ordered to pay $300,000 in damages to a former Chicago Bulls cheerleader he injured during a performance.

Yes, there is a Crazyball sense of invincibility when he gets into costume.

"Sometimes, I think when I'm wearing this chicken suit I can live forever. I'm not kidding, man," he once told The Associated Press. "I'm the class clown, and I have the whole ballpark as my room."

THE STANFORD TREE

Once described by the archrivals from Cal as looking like "a constipated squid struggling with dinner," the Tree does have a confounding presence. It's not even an official mascot for the Palo Alto, California, university. It is instead a member of the Stanford Band, representative of El Palo Alto, the Redwood tree that is the logo of the city of Palo Alto.

And it sure can ruffle the leaves of opponents.

Before the 2011 Orange Bowl against Virginia Tech, the Tree grabbed a hatchet the Hokies' Turkey planned to use to chop down the pride of Stanford, broke it over his, uh, trunk, and deposited it in a garbage can. The Turkey quickly waved good-bye, no longer interested in any interaction.

The Tree, which continually made national news for misbehavior, was at it again in an altercation at the 2006 NCAA women's basketball tournament.

The Tree was banned from appearing at the next year's tourney.

"I sort of look at the NCAA like an ex-girlfriend trying to come and take the boom box back or something," said Tom Leep, the student inside the bark at that time.

Leep remained in character when he was chased from the court during that tournament game in Denver. He was seen dancing in the Pepsi Arena tunnel as NCAA officials chided him—with national TV cameras capturing it all.

Coach Tara VanDerveer was upset—with the Tree.

"The band has always been kind of a free-spirit group, but that night, they showed more of the Tree on TV than they did of our win against Florida State, and that hurts our team."

OTTO THE ORANGE

Oh, Otto, how could ESPN be so down on you?

The Syracuse Orange once was voted among the worst mascots of March Madness by the network. That, in itself, is simply madness.

Otto was dubbed "a furry (moldy?), often-deformed orange with an insipid smile" by ESPN. We see him as a lovable piece of fruit with no chance of surviving a Syracuse winter if he was real. In 1995 he even got through a near-purge by the school chancellor, who appointed a committee to find a replacement, only to have the students rebel in support of their sacred citrus.

How popular has Otto become in upstate New York, to ESPN's disapproval? In 2013, Turning Stone Casino and Resort in nearby Verona brought in Wei-Sen Liang, a local award-winning sculptor, to make a 12-foot ice sculpture of Otto when the Orange made the Final Four in basketball.

Predicted Liang to the *Syracuse Post-Standard*, "If I can win first place, so can Syracuse."

The Orange didn't, and Otto's ice likeness melted.

HARVEY THE HOUND

Harvey doesn't make our honor roll for any distinguishing features, but for one incident that will forever be in the Mascot Hall of Shame.

Not that Harvey isn't memorable with his white boots and upper body, red pants, gold belt, and long red tongue. Ah, the tongue.

During a Calgary Flames game against archrival Edmonton in 2003, Harvey was doing his thing behind the Oilers bench, inciting the crowd during a timeout. He also incited Oilers coach Craig MacTavish.

Moments later, as Harvey leaned over the glass separating the players from the crowd, MacTavish reached up, yanked on the tongue, and ripped it out. He then flipped it back into the crowd as a stunned Harvey looked on.

No longer interested in being man's best friend—at least not MacTavish's best friend—Harvey leaned over the glass again, and MacTavish reached for a hockey stick. He was stopped by the Oilers' trainer while several players squirted Harvey with water bottles.

Not to be outdone, the hound came out during the intermission with a long red scarf replacing the tongue, extending from inside his mouth down to about his knees. He even found a way to keep the scarf protruding from his mouth while rapping the other end of it on his shoulder.

Sadly, Harvey's career was interrupted by the awful floods in Alberta during the summer of 2013. Workers cleaning a flooded Saddledome discovered his head floating in the mess.

According to the Calgary Sun, one worker said: "It scared the hell out of me. His eyes staring at me was creepy."

THE GORILLA

Don't try this one at home, unless your home is where the Phoenix Suns play and you are wearing a gorilla suit.

If you're looking for acrobatic mascots, it's difficult to top this whirling dervish. And the capper of his act: "Go" soars through a burning hoop to dunk two-handed into the basket.

The original Go, a Suns fan named Henry Rojas, had a job singing telegrams for a company called Eastern Onion (don't think Western Union was going to sue over that rip-off). Rojas got inventive when summoned to sing to someone in the crowd at a game.

"I was already visible in the suit and I thought I've got to make something out of it," he told azfamily.com. "They start to play music and I stop dead in my tracks, it's like I had no control over my feet, and shuffled on the court and started dancing."

From such early steps are mascot legends made.

Soon, the Gorilla was a regular attraction at Suns contests.

Go lists himself as 5-foot-ape, claims he went to Fur-man University, and has a weakness for bananas. A member of the Mascot Hall of Fame, he has performed in 17 countries and comes from a performing family—he alleges his dad starred alongside Charlton Heston in *Planet of the Apes*.

MILWAUKEE'S RACING SAUSAGES

Here's five for your money: Brat, Polish Sausage, Italian Sausage, Hot Dog, and Chorizo.

Considering they are fixtures at Milwaukee Brewers games sort of makes your mouth water, doesn't it?

But these particular foodies are elongated mascots who stage races at Miller Park. They have even raced against the Pittsburgh Pierogies in what could develop someday into a more heated rivalry than Pirates-Brewers ever will become.

As the Brewers mention on their website, Hideo Nomo, Pat Meares, and Geoff Jenkins "are just three of the lucky players to boast 'Racing Sausage' among their personal accolades."

Carrying the luscious legend further, the Brewers claim that Brat came to them "after years of Olympic training on the German National team, never quite making it past the trials."

Polish Sausage was a high school track coach. Italian Sausage made his fame in films, appearing in such low-budget cinema as *Sausages Are a Butcher's Best Friend* and *Sausages, Sausages, and More Sausages*.

Hot Dog, well, he is as American as a mascot can get and comes from a famous family that includes Cheese Dog, Chili Dog, Chicago Style Hot Dog, and Corn Dog.

And Chorizo, who joined the races full-time in 2007, brings some Latin spice to the festivities.

The on-field characters stem from scoreboard races between Brat and the two sausages. In two decades of racing, originally with just three meat products running wild, the fans have found the jaunts as entertaining as the baseball. Maybe more so, in some of the Brewers' down years.

Recalls Michael Dillon, winner of the first race, "You cannot imagine how insane that stadium went when we ran out there. It was so funny."

IZZY

This guy was a flop, a misguided creation for what was the most overhyped and overcommercialized Olympics, the 1996 Atlanta Games.

Izzy was such a failure that Bob Costas, not exactly known for razor-edged criticism, described him as "a genetic experiment gone horribly, ghastly wrong."

Every Olympic organizing committee before and after the Atlantans tended to go for the cuddly, warm, fuzzy mascot who would practically jump off the merchandising shelves directly into the arms of young (and older) fans.

Izzy repulsed. One publication wondered if it represented roadkill. Another suggested it was a character even Charlie Brown would beat up.

Whatizit was the official name, and "Whyizit the Games' mascot" became the central question.

Even the *New York Times*, hardly the forerunner of Deadspin, had some fun at Izzy's expense when it quoted sociologist John Shelton Reed about Izzy:

"In some ways, Izzy is an appropriate mascot because Atlanta doesn't know what it wants to be either, but you don't necessarily want to draw attention to that. You look for a mascot that has some cultural resonance or historical resonance that tells you you're in Atlanta instead of Denver or Dar es Salaam. With this, you don't know what it is. Hell, they don't even know what it is."

Enough said.

ICEBURGH

At 6-foot-4, 220 pounds, Iceburgh could be an enforcer for the Penguins. Then again, one look and you know this bird is a cream puff.

Complete with a lovably goofy smile, crossed eyes, and a baggy uniform, Iceburgh has been rooting on the Penguins since 1992. In 1995, his character, called Icey, was used as a disguise for a terrorist in the film *Sudden Death*. The movie's hero, Jean-Claude Van Damme, took care of Iceburgh and the rest of the criminals.

Generally, though, Iceburgh has been on good behavior. He loves to mix with the fans in the stands, sliding down banisters, dancing in the aisles, and giving high fives (or low fives, depending on the size) to fans.

He got his name from a contest conducted by Eat'n Park restaurants after Martha Johnson, wife of then-coach Bob Johnson, suggested his creation.

The original team mascot was a live penguin, Pete, but he died nine months after debuting in 1968. Undeterred, the Pens brought in another real penguin for the 1971-72 season.

"I remember that Pete died and that they brought in another one. They called the second one 'Re-Pete,'" said Penguins goaltender Les Binkley.

YOUPPI!

Poor Youppi! was abandoned by his team, the Expos.

Lucky Youppi! then caught on with merely the most successful franchise in Canadian sports, hockey's most dominant dynasty, Les Canadiens.

He was instantly dubbed "The Comeback King" in Montreal.

Youppi! spent a quarter-century supporting the Expos, who then hightailed it to Washington DC, leaving the orange-and-white-faced mascot every shade of blue.

But if he is anything, Youppi! is resilient. Months after the Expos left following the 2004 baseball season, the most-prized free agent in mascot history landed with the Canadiens. The hockey team, owner of a record 23 Stanley Cups, bought the rights to Youppi!, including the trademark exclamation point.

"I think it's wonderful that his tradition will live on here as a Canadien," said Gary Carter, one of the most popular players in Expo history and a baseball Hall of Famer. "He was always well-known, well-received, well-liked throughout all of baseball and everything, and he goes from one sport to the next. We know who the mascot is inside the mascot, so we knew that he could skate. I think he'll be a great representative."

When Youppi switched from balls to pucks and donned skates, he joined the Canadiens as a trendsetter, becoming the first mascot employed by two major league clubs.

And two years later, Youppi! became mayor of Youppi!ville, an area inside the Bell Centre where the Canadiens play.

Like nearly every mascot, Youppi! has his sweet, entertaining side. And like many such characters, he also has his darker moments.

During a marathon 22-inning game with the Dodgers, Youppi!, dressed in a nightgown, began dancing atop the LA dugout. The manager who began protesting the mascot's presence—as with the Phanatic in Philadelphia—was Tommy Lasorda. He persuaded umpire Bob Davidson to toss Youppi!!!!

Even worse, Youppi! was slugged by a slugger. As Pierre Deschenes, who played the Hall of Fame character from 1989–1992, told The Associated Press:

"We always would ring a bell when George Bell came to town, so he was in a bad mood, usually, to begin with. Then, I pick up his hat and glove. And when he finds out it is me, he punches me hard in my nose.

"To this day, I don't know if he means to hurt me or not," added Deschenes, who has taught at a mascot school. "But that's why I always tell students, 'Have some limits. Be nice with people so they will make nice back.' But above all 'stay on your toes.'"

Good advice—except for our final mascot.

BANANA SLUG

It's impossible to stay on your toes when you have none. So, with variations to his anatomy, the Banana Slug of California-Santa Cruz has found a way to survive and prosper since 1986, when he became the official mascot of the school.

Described by Santa Cruz officials as "a bright yellow, slimy, shell-less mollusk commonly found on the redwood forest floor," this mascot actually does walk around to perform his havoc. You didn't really expect him to do any damage, or entertain many fans, while crawling, did you?

"Our mascot is so ridiculously wacky that it's inspiring," says Carrie Osgood, a California-Santa Cruz graduate. "The lack of competitive focus, combined with a deep value of learning and reflection, contributes to why we love our mascot so much. The Banana Slug emphasizes creativity, ingenuity, and slowing down to appreciate all that makes life interesting and compelling. And it's funny!

"Just walking into the bookstore with all of the slug gear—from fuzzy slug slippers to glow-in-the-dark slugs to slimy slugs to the huge variety of traditional to silly logos, one has to smile in response."

Reader's Digest certainly smiled on Santa Cruz in 2004 when it plugged the Slug as the nation's best mascot, beating out even the Phanatic (we disagree, but we digress). Their reasoning:

"In 1965, students chose the bright yellow mollusk, native to the region, to protest the fierce athletic competition at America's colleges. Win or lose, you still gotta laugh."

When students voted by a 5-to-1 margin to make Banana Slugs the school's nickname in 1986, ditching Sea Lions, then-Chancellor Robert Sinsheimer wrote, "As a symbol of our athletic ambitions, consider that the banana slug is spineless, yellow (cowardly), sluggish (slow of foot) and slimy (enough said)."

Still, even Jerry Garcia and the boys in the band were fans. The Grateful Dead's archives were given to the university in 2008.

Which means the Banana Slug was "Truckin'."

Santa Cruz had all sorts of options for replacing the Sea Lion, because raccoons, deer, even wild felines were native to the campus.

"But the most notable, of course, was the banana slug, which was most likely to be sighted after heavy rains, as they would slip off the trees and land in the paths," Osgood recalls. "Whenever anyone saw one, which wasn't frequent, we would usually pause to appreciate the beloved slimy yellow mollusk. It was the same color and shape as one of the leaves that would fall in the forest, so despite their bright yellow color, they did blend into the natural environment.

"A freshman rite of passage was seeing one's first banana slug on campus. And it was always sad when we saw a dead, smooshed slug that was run over by bicyclists.

"Even after graduation, I went hiking with a friend who still lived in the area and when we saw a slug off the trail, we had to stop and take a photo."

Once a Slug, always a Slug.

12

SAY WHAT?

Any examination of sports' great double-talkers has to begin and end with Casey Stengel and Yogi Berra.

A conversation with the great manager of the Dodgers, Braves, Yankees, and Mets never really was a conversation at all. It was an oratory in Stengelese.

And it featured such perplexing pronouncements as:

- "All right everyone, line up alphabetically according to your height."
- "There comes a time in every man's life, and I've had plenty of them."
- "Being with a woman all night never hurt no professional baseball player. It's staying up all night looking for a woman that does him in."
- "If we're going to win the pennant, we've got to start thinking we're not as good as we think we are."

Perhaps Stengel's soliloquies or rantings were sparked by a simple question such as, "How does your catching situation look?"

And off Stengel went, punctuating his remarks with this memorable description:

"I got one that can throw but can't catch, and one that can catch but can't throw, and one who can hit but can't do either."

He couldn't recall their names.

Certainly, none of them was named Yogi. Like Stengel, Berra was a Hall of Famer, versatile enough to squat behind the plate or play a solid outfield.

And so versatile with the tongue that Yogisms became part of the American vernacular.

Such as (take a deep breath):

- "Nobody goes there anymore, it's too crowded."
- "When you come to a fork in the road, take it."
- "Baseball is ninety percent mental. The other half is physical."
- "He hits from both sides of the plate. He's amphibious."
- "A nickel ain't worth a dime anymore."

Casey and Yogi. Quite a pair, but hardly the only masters of the wise-guy quote in sports. On the fields, courts, rinks, and links, you can find them.

We did.

BASEBALL

The hefty John Kruk on his livelihood:

"I'm not an athlete. I'm a professional baseball player."

Irreverent relief pitcher Tug McGraw on whether he liked the surface at the Houston Astrodome:

"I don't know. I never smoked any Astroturf."

Chicago White Sox owner Eddie Einhorn on procuring talent:

"I told [general manager] Roland Hemond to go out and get me a big name pitcher. He said, 'Dave Wehrmeister's got 11 letters. Is that a big enough name for you?'"

FOOTBALL

New Orleans Saints running back George Rogers was asked about an upcoming season:

"I want to rush for 1,000 or 1,500 yards, whichever comes first."

Former player turned commentator Joe Theismann about the brainpower of coaches:

"Nobody in football should be called a genius. A genius is a guy like Norman Einstein."

LSU coach Les Miles evaluating the previous season:

"I think last year was a year like many years that will come and be there in the future."

Rich Kotite on ending his error, uh, era in charge and no longer being coach of the New York Jets:

"I was not fired, I am not quitting."

But he was out after a 4-27 record.

BASKETBALL

Chuck Nevitt, North Carolina State center, telling coach Jim Valvano why he struggled with nerves during a practice:

"My sister's expecting a baby, and I don't know if I'm going to be an uncle or an aunt."

Frank Layden, then president of the Utah Jazz, about a player who just didn't get it:

"Son, what is it with you? Is it ignorance or apathy?" He said, 'Coach, I don't know and I don't care.'"

Hall of Fame coach Red Auerbach on his skill set:

"I have two college degrees, but the only way I could make a living was by showing kids how to put a ball in a hole."

SOCCER

German national team star Lukas Podolski on the unpredictable nature of his sport:

"Soccer is like chess, but without the dice."

Swedish star Freddie Ljungberg on abstaining before matches:

"I usually don't have sex. Not on the same day. I say 'No, thanks.' I guess that, mentally, I want to keep the feeling in my feet and that's why. I think the feeling sort of disappears out of your feet if you have sex before. I have tried before and my feet felt like concrete when you are supposed to kick the ball."

Former Italy coach Giovanni Trapattoni on his team being down in the dumps:

"We can't behave like crocodiles and cry over spilled milk and broken eggs."

AUTO RACING

Kurt Busch after winning NASCAR's Oscar Mayer Wienermobile race at Charlotte, North Carolina:

"My wiener has never been so exhausted."

1992 Winston Cup champion Alan Kulwicki on the difference between night racing and day racing:

"It's basically the same, just darker."

Hall of Fame driver Darrell Waltrip:

"If you don't cheat, you look like an idiot; if you cheat and don't get caught, you look like a hero; if you cheat and get caught, you look like a dope. Put me where I belong."

HOCKEY

Career victories leader Martin Brodeur, the New Jersey Devils' three-time Cup-winning goalie:

"Why is a puck called a puck? Because dirty little bastard was taken."

NHL forward Petr Klima on why he broke his sticks after scoring:

"I only have one goal in each stick."

Rangers goalie Bob Froese after fans threw mugs on the ice during Mug Night:

"I'm just glad it wasn't Machete Night."

Forward/enforcer Stu Grimson on why he kept a color photograph of himself above his locker:

"That's so when I forget how to spell my name, I can still find my clothes."

Capitals coach Tom McVie on how he handled a loss:

"I slept like a baby. Every two hours I woke up and cried."

GOLF

Winston Churchill on his disdain for the sport:

"Golf is a game whose aim is to hit a very small ball into an even smaller hole, with weapons singularly ill-designed for the purpose."

The Rev. Billy Graham:

"The only time my prayers are never answered is on the golf course."

Baseball Hall of Famer Hank Aaron on hitting the links:

"It took me 17 years to get 3,000 hits in baseball. I did it in one afternoon on the golf course."

Two-time Masters champion Ben Crenshaw on how much better he could have been:

"I'm about five inches from being an outstanding golfer. That's the distance my left ear is from my right."

TENNIS

Martina Navratilova going out on a limb:

"I had a feeling today that Venus Williams would either win or lose."

Hall of Famer Billie Jean King summing up her sport:

"Tennis is a perfect combination of violent action taking place in an atmosphere of total tranquility."

Rocker Jon Bon Jovi on the best use for a racquet:

"I was just another long-haired teenage kid with visions of grandeur, strumming a tennis racket or a broom in front of his bedroom mirror."

HORSE RACING

Actor Robert Morley on the business of the sport of kings:

"There is little to compare with the thrill of standing next to the creature in the winner's enclosure, avoiding his hooves and receiving the congratulations of the press, your trainer, and friends who backed it. What makes the experience so satisfying is that you, the owner, have had absolutely nothing to do with the horse winning."

Comedian Danny Thomas on the art of betting the horses:

"A racetrack is a place where windows clean people."

Pro Football Hall of Famer Dick Butkus on life after the game:

"If I were young, fast, healthy, and had a lot of money and my whole sex life ahead of me, I'd retire—like Secretariat."